T0368861

THE NEW TEACHER'S GUIDE TO OFSTED

Sara Miller McCune founded SAGE Publishing in 1965 to support the dissemination of usable knowledge and educate a global community. SAGE publishes more than 1000 journals and over 800 new books each year, spanning a wide range of subject areas. Our growing selection of library products includes archives, data, case studies and video. SAGE remains majority owned by our founder and after her lifetime will become owned by a charitable trust that secures the company's continued independence.

Los Angeles | London | New Delhi | Singapore | Washington DC | Melbourne

SAMUEL STONES AND JONATHAN GLAZZARD

THE NEW TEACHER'S GUIDE TO OFSTED

THE **2019** EDUCATION INSPECTION FRAMEWORK

Learning Matters
A SAGE Publishing Company
1 Oliver's Yard
55 City Road
London EC1Y 1SP

SAGE Publications Inc.
2455 Teller Road
Thousand Oaks, California 91320

SAGE Publications India Pvt Ltd
B 1/I 1 Mohan Cooperative Industrial Area
Mathura Road
New Delhi 110 044

SAGE Publications Asia-Pacific Pte Ltd
3 Church Street
#10-04 Samsung Hub
Singapore 049483

Editor: Amy Thornton
Senior project editor: Chris Marke
Marketing manager: Lorna Patkai
Cover design: Wendy Scott
Typeset by: C&M Digitals (P) Ltd, Chennai, India
Printed in the UK

Library of Congress Control Number: 2020933767

British Library Cataloguing in Publication Data

A catalogue record for this book is available from the British Library

ISBN 978-1-5297-1210-0
ISBN 978-1-5297-1209-4 (pbk)

At SAGE we take sustainability seriously. Most of our products are printed in the UK using responsibly sourced papers and boards. When we print overseas we ensure sustainable papers are used as measured by the PREPS grading system. We undertake an annual audit to monitor our sustainability.

CONTENTS

ABOUT THE AUTHORS

Samuel Stones is a doctoral student, lecturer and researcher in the Carnegie School of Education at Leeds Beckett University. His research outputs are linked with the Centre for LGBTQ+ Inclusion in Education and the Carnegie Centre of Excellence for Mental Health in Schools. Samuel currently supervises dissertation students on a range of postgraduate courses and he works with initial teacher training students in university and school contexts. Samuel also holds a national training role for a Multi-Academy Trust and is also an Associate Leader and Head of Year at a secondary school and sixth form college in North Yorkshire.

Jonathan Glazzard is Professor of Inclusive Education at Leeds Beckett University. He is the professor attached to the Carnegie Centre of Excellence for Mental Health in Schools. Professor Glazzard teaches across a range of QTS and non-QTS programmes, and is an experienced teacher educator having previously been head of academic development at Leeds Trinity University and head of primary initial teacher training courses at the University of Huddersfield. Jonathan is a qualified teacher and taught in primary schools before moving into higher education.

INTRODUCTION

School inspections can be challenging for school leaders and teachers. They can be particularly challenging for early career teachers who may be facing an inspection for the first time. This book outlines the expectations of the new Education Inspection Framework (Ofsted, 2019) that was introduced in September 2019.

It is interesting to consider the new framework within the context of its predecessor. Some people may feel that the new framework is radically different from the old framework, while others may believe that this is a process of evolution. Previous inspection frameworks have focused on evaluating schools based on academic standards. The attainment of learners in relation to nationally expected standards of attainment has largely determined school inspection judgements, and this has, in some schools, impacted detrimentally on the quality of the education that learners receive. In recent years, we have witnessed the marginalisation of subjects that have not been tested. Schools have focused largely on subjects that are assessed. This narrowing of the curriculum has resulted in learners studying a restricted curriculum. They have been denied their entitlement to a broad, rich and balanced curriculum and this has meant that students are often unprepared to cope with the demands of their next steps. Restricting access to a broad curriculum impacts detrimentally on learners' mental health and results in their talents not being recognised.

Previous inspection frameworks have in many cases led to the narrowing of the curriculum. In a drive to raise academic standards in the subjects that have been assessed, effective pedagogy has also been a casualty. Some schools have accelerated academic attainment by teaching to the test. Teachers have prioritised teaching examination techniques through completing exam-style questions and learners have been required to understand the expectations of mark schemes.

Within this context, it is unsurprising when learners disengage from their education. Too many young people have been let down by an education system that has privileged academic attainment above learning for enjoyment. Those learners who excel in subjects such as music, art and the humanities have not been given enough opportunities to demonstrate their strengths, and the limited time that has been allocated to the broader, rich curriculum has resulted in learners not being able to study the foundation subjects in depth. The teaching of the foundation subjects in primary schools has been largely superficial. Teachers have covered key subject content in a limited time, resulting in learners being denied valuable opportunities to investigate and explore subjects in depth. Teachers have prioritised assessment in the core subjects, resulting in assessment in the foundation subjects being superficial, weak or non-existent. The National Curriculum does not specify national standards in the foundation subjects and therefore schools have had to determine their own standards. This has had a detrimental impact on curriculum planning because teachers have not been provided with guidance that specifies what knowledge and skills learners should develop by specific ages.

In addition, in primary schools many of the foundation subjects have been taught through cross-curricular or thematic approaches. Although these approaches to curriculum planning can help learners to make meaningful connections between subjects, they have also resulted in insufficient focus on the subject-specific knowledge and skills that learners need to be taught. In addition, thematic approaches to planning can also have a detrimental impact on planning for progression in knowledge and skills unless themes are very carefully planned.

In secondary schools, curriculum marginalisation has continued with greater curriculum time being allocated to subjects that determine inspection outcomes. The emphasis on academic attainment has resulted in a range of detrimental effects. Teachers have focused on teaching to examinations, and in some schools GCSE programmes have commenced in Year 9 rather than Year 10 to increase results. Increasing numbers of young people have experienced 'off-rolling'. They have been moved to other schools because of the potential detrimental impact that their behaviour or academic outcomes can have on a school's academic profile. This has had a damaging impact on their self-esteem and confidence, but it has allowed the school to maintain its results.

The impact of previous inspection frameworks has also affected teachers. The pressure on schools to raise academic attainment has created, in some schools, toxic workplace cultures. Teachers currently experience significant workload-related stress. There has been an emphasis on producing evidence for inspectors that has led to increasing amounts of paperwork that has had minimal positive impacts on learners. Teachers in England and worldwide currently experience significant workload-related stress and burnout. In addition, there is a problem with teacher retention. Far too many teachers leave teaching within the first five years of teaching, and teachers at all stages of their careers experience stress and depression. The Education Support Partnership has researched the well-being of education professionals for the past three years and the outcomes of their research makes grim reading. In some schools, teachers have been subjected to workplace bullying, harassment and discrimination from school leaders. Toxic cultures have been created in some schools that have restricted teacher agency, undermined their professionalism and damaged their efficacy. Increasing numbers of teachers have lost their jobs at the hands of school leaders who have not demonstrated compassionate leadership.

It could be argued that the focus on attainment outcomes in previous inspection frameworks have led to these detrimental effects. This bleak picture is certainly not evident in all schools. The best schools have retained their focus on learners' holistic well-being. They have prioritised effective pedagogy over test results and they have provided learners with a broad, rich, creative and stimulating curriculum.

The new Education Inspection Framework provides an opportunity for schools to reclaim the curriculum and high-quality pedagogy. The focus is on the curriculum – the real substance of education. Inspectors will pay less attention to school examination results and will give greater attention to the quality of the curriculum. Inspectors will look in-depth at curriculum plans in a broad range of subjects through 'deep dives'. There will be a greater focus on how knowledge and skills are sequenced across units of work, across year groups and across Key Stages. There will be an enhanced emphasis on what students are learning and the depth at which they study subjects. Inspectors will pay much greater attention to the rationale that underpins the curriculum plan, and they will evaluate whether the curriculum is ambitious and provides learners with cultural capital.

Inspectors will also examine the school culture. They will ask staff about workplace bullying and they will evaluate the extent to which school leaders have made genuine attempts to reduce teacher workload. Evidence of 'off-rolling' learners to other schools will have a detrimental effect on school inspection judgements.

The framework is refreshing. It appears to focus on what matters most – the quality of students' education. It provides an exciting opportunity for schools to reclaim the curriculum. Although schools are still expected to teach the National Curriculum, the framework will evaluate the extent to which the school curriculum meets the needs of the school's context and the community which the schools serve. This provides an opportunity for schools to tailor the curriculum to respond to its learners and the community.

This book introduces the Education Inspection Framework. It is targeted at early career teachers. Chapter 1 introduces the framework and outlines what inspection means for teachers. Chapter 2 covers the myths that are associated with inspection. Chapter 3 examines effective pedagogical approaches that are research informed. The remaining chapters address each of the four aspects of the framework: the quality of education; behaviour and attitudes; personal development, and leadership and management. These chapters outline the expectations of the framework and provide practical guidance to school leaders and teachers. In Chapter 4 we explain what is meant by cultural capital and explore ways of embedding this into the curriculum. The final chapter synthesises the key messages from the preceding chapters.

Inspection is nothing to worry about. If you are doing a consistently good job, then you do not need to be concerned by inspection. Inspectors rarely seek to catch you out. They are simply there to evaluate the quality of education that students receive. You do not need to invest copious amounts of time preparing for an inspection. If you are doing your job consistently well, then you will already have the evidence that you need. Inspectors will observe lessons, talk to learners, look at their work, talk to subjects and senior leaders. They are interested in the quality of students' education, what they are taught and how well it is planned and taught. A well-constructed, broad, rich and meaningful curriculum should produce good educational outcomes. Inspectors will evaluate the curriculum intent, implementation and impact. They will not expect everything to be perfect. They will be interested in whether you have identified any areas for development and whether you are addressing these. Schools are always 'a work in progress'. You are on a journey. You will not be expected to reach a destination.

We have provided within each chapter opportunities for you to reflect on your own practice. We have also integrated case studies of practice into each chapter to exemplify and illuminate best practice.

1

WHAT DOES OFSTED MEAN FOR TEACHERS?

WHAT WILL YOU LEARN?

This chapter introduces the Education Inspection Framework (Ofsted, 2019) and outlines its four key aspects in relation to the judgements that will be made by inspectors. It also highlights the implications of these for school leadership teams and teachers. Additionally, the chapter considers the new inspection framework within the context of its predecessor and in doing so provides a summary of key changes. Some common myths and misconceptions are addressed, and practical guidance is offered in relation to the inspection process and your lesson planning. Throughout the chapter we draw on key research to illuminate examples of best practice and we illustrate these through practical, hands-on case studies to support your reflection on professional practice. The chapter also emphasises the importance of teachers' subject knowledge and the way in which this is presented to learners. There is discussion in relation to the role and value of assessment, and we situate this discussion within the context of the new inspection framework to support leaders and teachers with their understanding of the inspection and its implications. Finally, the chapter emphasises the importance of teachers and leaders working together to create a calm and safe learning environment and it begins to consider what this might look like in a range of educational contexts.

KEY POLICY

The Education Inspection Framework applies to maintained schools and academies, non-association independent schools, further education and skills providers, and early years settings. It is the framework that inspectors use to determine the quality of a setting. Judgements are applied to four key aspects:

- the quality of education;

- behaviour and attitudes;

- personal development;

- leadership and management.

The judgements made by inspectors in relation to each of these categories determines the overall inspection outcome for the school. Although school leadership teams influence all of the four aspects, teachers are also accountable for the quality of education, the behaviour and attitudes of learners and their personal development, regardless of the stage they are at in their career.

Inspectors quality assure the school provision to determine the quality of education that is provided. Previous inspection frameworks have focused heavily on the outcomes that learners achieve. This has resulted in schools focusing on raising academic attainment, often at the expense of the quality of the education that schools provide. The current inspection framework focuses much more sharply on the curriculum as the underpinning 'substance of education' (Spielman, 2019). Schools and teachers therefore need to give attention to what learners are being taught, how well they are being taught and what learners know and can do as a result of the curriculum. Inspectors will focus on the richness of the curriculum and there will be less focus on paperwork that is generated solely for the purposes of inspections.

The new framework provides a refreshing opportunity for schools to reclaim the curriculum. Although there is an expectation that learners will be taught the National Curriculum, there is a greater focus on the ways in which schools shape the curriculum to suit their own contexts. This ensures that the curriculum provides learners with rich, meaningful and relevant learning opportunities which provide them with cultural capital. This concept will be further explored in Chapter 4.

WHAT DOES INSPECTION MEAN FOR ME?

Inspectors are not looking for a 'show pony'. This is a teacher who is able to perform well during observations, but when they are not being observed their performance is inadequate. Neither are they looking for a 'jazz hands' type of teacher – one who is all-singing and all-dancing during observations but lifeless the rest of the time. What inspectors are looking for is an effective teacher who can promote learning – that is, they ensure that learners gain knowledge, skills and understanding. Inspection is not about 'putting on a show'. If you teach effectively consistently, then you have nothing to worry about. Inspectors are not trying to catch you out. They seek assurances, through lesson observations, talking to learners and looking at their work, that you are providing them with a consistently high-quality educational experience.

LESSON PLANNING

Inspectors will not expect to see lesson planning in a particular format. They will be more interested in how you are *sequencing* learning over time so that learners make gains in knowledge, skills and understanding. They are also interested in how you plan opportunities for learners to revisit concepts and skills over time so that they do not forget what you have taught them.

Inspectors will be able to ascertain from observing a lesson if the lesson is well planned. They do not need to see a lesson plan to make this judgement. This has implications for the way that you structure a lesson. Although inspectors will not expect to see a specific model of teaching, a well-structured lesson will include the following:

- checking on learners' understanding of what they have previously been taught;

- modelling and explaining new learning;

- opportunities for guided and independent practice;

- carefully sequenced lesson content to enable learners to make progress;

- use of assessment at specific points during the lesson.

KEY RESEARCH

Research identifies two evidence-informed strategies that support learning:

- **Spacing out learning:** According to Coe et al. (2014), *time spent reviewing or practising leads to much greater long-term retention if it is spread out, with gaps in between to allow forgetting.*

- **Interleaving:** According to Coe et al. (2014), *learning in a single block can create better immediate performance and higher confidence but interleaving with other tasks or topics leads to better long-term retention and transfer of skills.*

CASE STUDY

Sarah is an experienced middle leader and Head of Science in a large comprehensive school in North Yorkshire. Her colleague, Jasmin, is a recently appointed middle leader and Head of Maths. Their school has implemented a development programme to support new and aspiring middle leaders. This programme provides opportunities for middle leaders to work together to support and enhance professional development. In line with the school's teaching and learning priorities, Sarah and Jasmin have committed to a teaching and learning project that is designed to enhance and develop the existing Key Stage 3 curriculum offer within their subject areas.

With the support of the senior leaders, Sarah and Jasmin have dedicated some of their existing teaching and learning time to enable them to undertake this cross-curricular project. They have consulted with the teachers in their departments and have agreed that together they need to develop further their approaches to interleaving within and across their curriculum areas. The middle leaders have created a shared document that is accessible to all teachers within their departments. This document contains information in relation to common topics and concepts that are taught within the Key Stage 3 curriculum of each subject. Subject teachers can contribute to this document on an ongoing basis.

Sarah and Jasmin used this document to update their existing long-term curriculum plans. Together they identified the ways in which the skills and concepts of one subject could be taught, assessed or built upon within the context of the other subject. They also incorporated these common concepts in their assessment materials to support students in accessing and retrieving information. In one example, Jasmin was able to create and share a maths assessment which assessed the required mathematical skills, but through the presentation of a case study which students had been exposed to in an earlier science lesson. In another example, the teachers in Sarah's department were able to teach a problem-based lesson through developing students' understanding of ratios that had been taught in an earlier maths lesson. Through this collaboration, Sarah and Jasmin updated their existing curriculum plans in order to identify appropriate points to revisit the skills, concepts and knowledge taught in one another's subject areas.

To review the impact of their curriculum project, Sarah and Jasmin combined one of their faculty meetings. This provided an opportunity for all teachers of maths and science to jointly discuss and review the curriculum project. Within this meeting, one colleague explained that she was concerned that in some cases subject terminology differed in its meaning across subject areas. To address this challenge, the teachers worked together to identify concepts and vocabulary that differed in their application to the subject area. This information is now used by all teachers so that subject-specific differences can be explicitly taught and sequenced at appropriate points in the curriculum, regardless of a teacher's subject specialism.

A WELL-STRUCTURED LESSON WILL INCLUDE. . .

CHECKING ON LEARNERS' UNDERSTANDING OF WHAT THEY HAVE PREVIOUSLY BEEN TAUGHT

MODELLING & EXPLAINING NEW LEARNING

OPPORTUNITIES FOR GUIDED AND INDEPENDENT PRACTICE

CAREFULLY SEQUENCED LESSON CONTENT TO ENABLE LEARNERS TO MAKE PROGRESS

USE OF ASSESSMENT AT SPECIFIC POINTS DURING THE LESSON

SUBJECT KNOWLEDGE

Good subject knowledge is essential for effective teaching and learning. This requires that you understand not only the subject content of the lesson, but also understand what comes before and after that content within a sequence of learning. If you understand how your lesson fits into a sequence of lessons, you will be able to revisit prior learning if learners develop misconceptions and move them on to the next stage if they require additional challenge. Good subject knowledge also involves being aware of the likely misconceptions that learners may develop within a lesson. If you are aware of these, then you can specifically address them with your learners in the lesson.

Developing learners' subject-specific vocabulary is critical because advanced vocabulary provides learners with cultural capital. Identify opportunities within your lesson to explicitly teach subject-specific vocabulary and ensure that unfamiliar vocabulary within texts is explained to learners, as this will support their comprehension of a text.

KEY RESEARCH

According to Coe et al.:

The most effective teachers have deep knowledge of the subjects they teach, and when teachers' knowledge falls below a certain level it is a significant impediment to students' learning. As well as a strong understanding of the material being taught, teachers must also understand the ways students think about the content, be able to evaluate the thinking behind students' own methods and identify students' common misconceptions.

(Coe et al., 2014, p2)

PRESENTING SUBJECT MATTER

Inspectors will be interested in how you present subject matter to your learners. Clear, concise explanations are crucial, but it is also important to model new learning and tasks visually. Strategies to aid modelling include the following:

- sharing worked examples with learners on the interactive whiteboard;

- using a visualiser to live model a skill or task;

- presenting the solutions to a task on the board after learners have had an opportunity to practise the new learning independently, thus providing them with instant feedback;

- using a visualiser to live mark a piece of work, thus enabling learners to mark their own work after the marking process has been modelled.

The use of 'I', 'We', 'You' is also a useful strategy because it provides learners with additional support before they are required to complete a task independently. This strategy is summarised below:

I: Teacher models the new learning.

We: Guided practice in which learners work in pairs or groups to complete a task similar to the one that the teacher modelled or where the teacher provides learners with an opportunity to instruct the teacher how to complete a problem.

You: Independent practice – learners work silently.

KEY RESEARCH

Rosenshine has developed a set of principles that underpin effective instruction. In summary, the ten principles are as follows.

1. *Begin a lesson with a short review of previous learning.*

2. *Present new material in small steps, with pupil practice after each step.*

3. *Ask a large number of questions and check the responses of all pupils.*

4. *Provide models for problem solving and worked examples.*

5. *Guide pupil practice.*

6. *Check for pupil understanding.*

7. *Obtain a high success rate.*

8. *Provide scaffolds for difficult tasks.*

9. *Require and monitor independent practice.*

10. *Engage pupils in weekly and monthly review.*

(Rosenshine, 2010, 2012)

USING ASSESSMENT

Inspectors will be interested in the way in which you use assessment during the lesson to check understanding and promote learning. Assessment for Learning (AfL), or formative assessment, is assessment that promotes learning and informs planning and teaching. It is often informal and takes place within and between lessons.

Examples of strategies include noticing and responding to misconceptions, questioning, marking and feedback, quizzes, self- and peer-assessment, and talking to learners about what they are learning. It contrasts with Assessment of Learning (AoL), which is a summary of a learner's achievements at a specific point in time. It is usually formal and often takes the form of tests or examinations.

Inspectors are often critical of teachers who fail to pitch the subject content at the correct level for learners, resulting in content being too challenging or too easy. Knowing learners' starting points enables you to accurately pitch the work at the correct level. Inspectors are also critical of teachers who move on too quickly in lessons without stopping and checking learners' understanding. This results in learners being set tasks they do not understand.

Effective teachers can adapt their lessons to meet the needs of learners. They can quickly spot misconceptions and rectify these so that learners can make greater progress. They integrate assessment tasks into the lesson at specific stages to enable them to check learners' understanding before moving on.

Most teachers spend significant time marking work and writing feedback for learners. This can be deeply frustrating when learners do not take any notice of the feedback and continue making the same errors. Inspectors will be interested in how learners utilise feedback to make greater progress in their learning. They will also be interested in how teachers are making use of marking to identify misconceptions, which then inform subsequent teaching. Inspectors will check that the school assessment policy is being consistently applied.

Inspectors will not expect that every piece of work is marked. They will check the school assessment policy and evaluate the extent to which it has been applied consistently in practice. Many schools are now developing marking policies that reduce the workload of teachers. It is good practice to provide learners with oral and written feedback during lessons. It is not necessary to mark every piece of work in-depth. An effective and efficient strategy is to sample learners' work after lessons to identify strengths and misconceptions. You do not need to look at the work of all students. Instead, you can select a cross-section of learners and sample their work. You can identify the misconceptions quickly from this sample and address them in the next lesson. You can also provide generic feedback to the whole class so that they are aware of the strengths and weaknesses of their work.

At the start of lessons, it is important to assess the learners' understanding of their prior learning. It is a good idea to plan a short, snappy assessment activity which provides you with feedback on their understanding before moving on to the new learning. You could provide them with a starter task on the board which is designed to check their understanding of what they learned in the previous lesson. You could also design a quiz which they complete through writing answers on mini-whiteboards. Additionally, you could provide them with a set of words and definitions; the learners work in groups to match words to definitions and these are then laid out on their tables so that you can see quickly if they have understood the prior learning. Sorting and matching activities using cards are useful ways of checking on understanding using an interactive approach. After you have modelled the new learning, you should plan in another assessment for a learning task to check their understanding of the new learning. This should provide you with feedback in relation to whether they have understood and are ready to work independently on practising the new learning or whether you need to reteach the content. You should move around the room providing oral and written feedback, noticing and responding to misconceptions. At the end of the lesson, the plenary activity should be designed as an assessment task to check their understanding.

KEY RESEARCH

According to seminal research from Black and Wiliam:

There is a body of firm evidence that formative assessment is an essential component of classroom work and that its development can raise standards of achievement. We know of no other way of raising standards for which such a strong prima facie case can be made.

(1998, p12)

Black and Wiliam (1998) emphasised that:

- *Feedback should focus on the quality of the work and include advice on how to improve it. It must avoid comparisons with other pupils.*

- *Formative assessment is particularly beneficial for low-achieving pupils.*

- *Pupils' self-assessment is an important and effective method of formative assessment, but only if pupils understand the overall intentions of the task.*

- *Providing time for pupils to respond to questions by thinking them through with their peers is essential.*

- *Frequent, short tests during a unit of work can provide useful feedback both to pupils and teachers rather than fewer, long tests. However, providing marks or grades rather than feedback is counterproductive as pupils will focus on these rather than the feedback.*

- *Effective teaching cannot be separated from formative assessment. Effective teachers use assessment during their teaching rather than teaching and assessing learning at a later point.*

- *A classroom culture which promotes questioning and deep thinking in which pupils learn from shared discussions with peers and teachers is essential to effective teaching.*

(Continued)

> (Continued)
>
> Research suggests that models of feedback should address three questions:
>
> *Where am I going? How am I going? and Where to next? The answers to these questions enhance learning when there is a discrepancy between what is understood and what is aimed to be understood. It can increase effort, motivation, or engagement to reduce this discrepancy, and/or it can increase cue searching and task processes that lead to understanding (thus reducing this discrepancy). Feedback is among the most critical influences on student learning. A major aim of the educative process is to assist in identifying these gaps ('How am I going?' relative to 'Where am I going?') and to provide remediation in the form of alternative or other steps ('Where to next?').*
>
> (Hattie and Timperley, 2007)

CASE STUDY

Jamiq is a Year 4 teacher with additional leadership responsibilities for teacher training and development. In one of his recent training and development sessions, he led an activity that was designed to support teachers' awareness of the range of different approaches to assessment that can be used within the classroom.

Jamiq advised his colleagues that he had recently delivered a sequence of lessons on human and physical geography. He explained that he wanted to check learners' understanding of the topic before proceeding with his teaching for the remainder of the sequence. Jamiq was also concerned that some learners held misconceptions in relation to the separation of and difference between physical and human features.

Jamiq worked with his colleagues to create a list of things he expected his learners to be able to recall and understand:

- the relationship of hot and cold areas of the world in relation to the Equator and the North and South Poles;
- a range of key physical features;
- a range of key human features;
- the difference between physical and human features.

Jamiq worked with his colleagues to design an assessment using a combination of assessment approaches. Jamiq led a discussion with his colleagues about a range of assessment approaches, including when they might and might not be appropriate. These included:

- multiple-choice questions;

- short-answer responses;

- identifying errors and mistakes;

- recognising fake news headlines;

- providing answers for which learners must write a question;

- placing a series of answers in the right order.

CREATING A LEARNING ENVIRONMENT

Inspectors will be interested in the learning environment in the classroom. Learning is more likely to be effective when the atmosphere in the classroom is calm and safe so that learners can concentrate on the tasks that they have been set. Greeting learners at the door sets the lesson off with a positive atmosphere. Using praise throughout the lesson to appreciate manners, good effort and good work helps learners to stay motivated throughout the lesson. Dealing swiftly with low-level disruption will ensure that poor behaviour is addressed and does not have a detrimental impact on learning. The way in which learners speak to each other is also crucial and inspectors will be interested in whether or not learners treat each other with respect.

The learning environment in the early years and early primary phase will look very different from what we are describing above. Effective early years and early primary environments provide rich opportunities for children to learn through play. However, there should also be opportunities for young learners to work independently on more formal tasks to develop concentration and to prepare them for more formal stages of education.

PROFESSIONAL REFLECTION

Within your own professional context, consider:

- how you explain unfamiliar vocabulary within texts to ensure that learners are supported with their ability to comprehend and understand;

- how frequently you use and vary your approaches to Assessment for Learning so that subject content is pitched at the correct level for learners;

- the way in which you share marks and grades to ensure that learners do not lose focus on the importance of understanding and responding to feedback.

NEXT STEPS

You should be able to predict when your school will be next inspected. Consider what you need to do next to ensure that you are ready for the inspection. Identify your strengths and areas for development and discuss these with colleagues in school. Work on addressing these. Seek advice from colleagues in school and on social media.

TAKE 5

- Focus on how to sequence learning across a series of lessons.

- Identify what you want learners to achieve by the end of a unit. Work backwards from this to plan the 'stepping stones' towards this end goal.

- Think carefully about how you will assess learning within lessons, at key points across a sequence of lessons and at the end of a unit.

- Research learners' misconceptions as you plan lessons and turn these into teaching points.

- Address interleaving within lessons.

WHAT HAVE YOU LEARNED?

This chapter has introduced the Education Inspection Framework and it has summarised its four key aspects in relation to the judgements that will be made as part of an inspection. The chapter has also highlighted the implications of the framework for school leadership teams and teachers. It has considered the new inspection framework through providing some comparison with its predecessor and in doing it has summarised many of the key changes. A range of common myths and misconceptions have been addressed and practical guidance has been offered to teachers in relation to the inspection process and their lesson planning. Throughout the chapter, key research has been considered to illuminate examples of best practice and it has illustrated these through practical, hands-on case studies to support your reflection on professional practice. Additionally, the chapter has emphasised the importance of teachers having good subject knowledge and the way in which this is presented to learners. There has been a discussion in relation to the role and value of assessment and this has been situated within the context of the new inspection framework to support leaders and teachers with their understanding of the inspection and its implications. Finally, the chapter has explained the importance of teachers and leaders working together to create a calm and safe learning environment and it has provided some reflection on what this might look like in a range of educational contexts.

FURTHER READING

Fletcher-Wood, H (2018) *Responsive Teaching*. London: David Fulton.

Stacey, S (2018) *Inquiry-Based Early Learning Environments*. Saint Paul, MN: Redleaf Press.

2

MYTH BUSTING

WHAT WILL YOU LEARN?

This chapter addresses the key myths that are typically associated with Ofsted inspections. It also addresses myths that relate to planning, teaching and assessment, and those in relation to the wider context of teaching and learning. Several common myths have also been addressed in relation to active learning, use of praise, deployment of teaching assistants and learning styles. Some case study material is provided to support you in reflecting on your current practice and to exemplify effective practice.

KEY POLICY

This chapter addresses the key messages in the Education Inspection Framework (2019). It also addresses the myth-busting guidance (Ofsted, 2018) that was published for the previous inspection framework. Although this guidance is no longer current because the framework has changed, we have made the assumption that much of the previous content in the myth-busting guidance will remain in place in the current inspection framework. We have not addressed all of the myths; instead, we have focused on the myths that relate to your role as an early career teacher.

MYTHS ABOUT INTENT

The Education Inspection Framework evaluates the quality of education through intent, implementation and impact. Intent focuses on the quality of the curriculum. Implementation addresses the quality of teaching and impact evaluates the gains that learners make in knowledge and skills.

Good intent addresses the following aspects:

- a curriculum that is ambitious for all pupils;

- a curriculum that is coherently planned and sequenced;

- a curriculum that is successfully adapted, designed and developed for pupils with special educational needs and/or disabilities;

- a curriculum that is broad and balanced for all pupils.

Schools do not need to write new statements of intent, adapt websites or restructure staffing to cover intent. Intent simply focuses on whether the curriculum is ambitious, coherently planned and sequenced. It also addresses the extent to which the curriculum is broad, balanced and inclusive. Inspectors will evaluate the curriculum offer in primary schools to ensure that children are provided with a broad and balanced curriculum, and have the opportunity to study the full range of subjects in the National Curriculum. In the secondary phase, intent focuses on the extent to which learners are able to study a strong academic core of subjects, including English Baccalaureate (EBacc) subjects. Inspectors will evaluate whether there is high academic/vocational/technical ambition for all pupils. Essentially, intent focuses on whether the curriculum includes the knowledge and skills that learners need, and whether these are sequenced in a logical order to ensure that they make progress.

LESSON PLANNING

Previous myth-busting guidance (Ofsted, 2018) stated that Ofsted does not require schools to provide individual lesson plans to inspectors. Equally, Ofsted does not require schools to provide previous lesson plans. Ofsted does not specify how planning should be set out, the length of time it should take or the amount of detail it should contain. Inspectors are interested in the effectiveness of planning rather than the form it takes. It is likely, given the focus on the sequencing of curriculum knowledge and skills in the Education Inspection Framework that inspectors will want to see long-term curriculum plans to enable them to evaluate this aspect of the curriculum.

GRADING OF LESSONS

Inspectors do not grade individual lessons. Instead, they make an overall judgement on the quality of education through evaluating the quality of the curriculum and the quality of the teaching overall in the school through its impact on gains in learners' knowledge and skills.

PUPILS' WORK

Previous myth-busting guidance (Ofsted, 2018) stated that inspectors do not expect to see a particular frequency or quantity of work in pupils' books or folders. Ofsted recognises that the amount of work in books and folders will depend on the subject being studied and the age and ability of the pupils.

ASSESSMENT AND MARKING

Inspectors will not expect to see that marking follows a particular model. They will also not expect to see evidence that every piece of work has been marked. Inspectors will be more interested in the school marking policy and the extent to which this is implemented consistently throughout the school. They will not expect teachers to write detailed feedback on students' work. Instead, they will evaluate whether the feedback that learners are provided with helps them to make further progress. Inspectors will explore whether students make use of the feedback to reframe misconceptions and make gains in knowledge and skills.

Previous myth-busting guidance stated that:

> *Ofsted recognises that marking and feedback to pupils, both written and oral, are important aspects of assessment. However, Ofsted does not expect to see any specific frequency, type or volume of marking and feedback; these are for the school to decide through its assessment policy. Marking and feedback should be consistent with that policy . . . . While inspectors will consider how written and oral feedback is used to promote learning, Ofsted does not expect to see any written record of oral feedback provided to pupils by teachers.*
>
> (Ofsted, 2018)

In the Education Inspection Framework there is a much greater emphasis on the use of assessment within lessons. Effective assessment within lessons enables teachers to check learners' understanding, identify and respond to misconceptions and adapt teaching where necessary. Guidance in the framework states that inspectors will evaluate the extent to which teachers *check learners' understanding systematically, identify misconceptions accurately and provide clear, direct feedback. In doing so, they respond and adapt their teaching as necessary, without unnecessarily elaborate or differentiated approaches* (Ofsted, 2019, p9).

As part of the judgement on leadership and management, inspectors will evaluate the extent to which leaders have reduced unnecessary workload for teachers. Marking policies that cause excessive and unnecessary workload for teachers will not be viewed favourably. Schools that have made a deliberate decision to reduce

the amount of written feedback that students are given will not be penalised under the new framework. If they have taken steps to increase the amount of live feedback that students are provided with during lessons, this will be viewed favourably.

Inspectors will evaluate the extent to which the assessment policy encourages retrieval of knowledge and skills through revisiting prior content. In addition, inspectors will evaluate how teachers assess what learners know and can do within units of work, but also how they check that knowledge and skills have been committed to students' long-term memories after units of work have been taught.

EVIDENCE FOR INSPECTION

Ofsted does not expect schools to provide evidence for inspection beyond that set out in the inspection handbook. Ofsted will take a range of evidence into account when making judgements. Judgements will be made through observing lessons, talking to leaders and pupils and looking at documentary evidence. However, unnecessary or extensive collections of marked pupils' work are not required for inspection. Inspectors do not require teachers to undertake additional work or to ask pupils to undertake work specifically for the inspection.

In the new framework, inspectors will focus much more extensively on what the school wants students to learn, how well it is taught, and the impact of the teaching through gains in knowledge and skills. Previous inspection frameworks have focused more extensively on outcomes for learners through evaluating their progress and attainment. This has resulted in a lack of emphasis on the quality of the education, and in many schools the focus on outcomes has led to curriculum narrowing and teaching to the test. In contrast, the current framework gives much greater emphasis on whether the curriculum is ambitious and logically sequenced so that the correct building blocks of knowledge and skills are secure at the right time. There is a greater emphasis on curriculum breadth and the extent to which the curriculum provides all learners with cultural capital. This is discussed in Chapter 4.

Previous myth-busting guidance (Ofsted, 2018) has also stated that:

- Ofsted does not require schools to provide evidence for each teacher for each of the bulleted subheadings in the teachers' standards. There is no expectation that individual teachers should maintain a file of evidence to demonstrate their achievement of the teachers' standards. This practice takes time away from the important tasks that are associated with being a teacher.

- Ofsted does not expect to see photographic evidence of pupils' work (or learning in action). Ofsted is very aware of teachers' workload and inspectors are happy to speak to pupils during an inspection about what they have learned.

This is particularly important guidance for teachers who work in the Early Years Foundation Stage who have become used to this practice. The amount of documentary evidence that teachers collect should be reasonable and limited to that which is necessary to help them make further progress. Time spent documenting learning and taking photographs of learning reduces the available time that teachers can spend interacting with children. Interacting with children is what makes the greatest difference to their learning.

- Ofsted does not require schools to retain students' books and other examples of students' work from the previous academic year.

- Ofsted does not require schools to predict their attainment and progress scores. It is impossible to predict attainment and progress as examination and test results for each cohort are compared nationally, and this cannot be done until after the examinations or tests.

- There is no expectation that schools need to have policies relating to staff behaviour in any particular format.

- The overall effectiveness judgement for an inspection does not predetermine the outcome of any subsequent inspection.

LESSON OBSERVATIONS

Ofsted does not require schools to undertake a specified number of lesson observations or to ensure that the monitoring of teaching is carried out in a specific way. Inspectors do not expect that lesson observations will be graded because it is not possible to grade a teacher on the basis of a single lesson observation. Inspectors will expect school leaders to be able to evaluate the quality of teaching within the school, but there is no expectation that this has to be based on lesson observations. Judgements on the quality of teaching can be made on the basis of a range of evidence, which may include learning walks, lesson observations, conversations with learners and teachers, assessment data and the quality of students' work.

TEACHING STYLE

Inspectors will not expect to see a specific model of lesson delivery. They do not expect lessons to follow a particular structure and they do not have any preconceived ideas about the balance between 'teacher talk' and independent learning within lessons. Therefore, the old myth of teachers only talking for a limited amount of time in lessons can be displaced. Inspectors are interested in the quality of teaching not the style of teaching. They will evaluate the extent to which the teaching results in gains in knowledge and skills. They will not expect to see starter activities and plenaries in lessons, and they will not expect that lessons are structured into a specified number of parts. Essentially, inspectors are only interested in the impact of the teaching on the quality of students' learning.

DIFFERENTIATION

The Education inspection Framework states that teachers should *check learners'* understanding systematically, identify misconceptions accurately and provide clear, direct feedback. In doing so, they respond and adapt their teaching as necessary, *without unnecessarily elaborate or differentiated approaches* (p9). Inspectors will not expect to see three, four or more levels of activities in lessons. Differentiation can have detrimental consequences. It can limit exposure to higher level knowledge and skills for specific learners, resulting in widening the ability gap. It can place a 'ceiling' on what specific learners know and are expected to do. It can be extremely time-consuming to plan multiple activities for learners to complete within lessons, and it can result in a culture of low expectations, particularly for learners with special educational needs and disabilities.

ACTIVE LEARNING

According to Coe et al. (2014), *Memory is the residue of thought ... so if you want students to remember something you have to get them to think about it. This might be achieved by being 'active' or 'passive'* (p24).

The myth that children need to be learning actively is not supported by research evidence. Although active learning can foster engagement, it is important to remember that active learning can reduce the pace of learning, resulting in inefficient use of lesson time. Children do not need to be 'doing things' to be actively learning. Direct instruction can promote active thinking which leads to learning. However, it is important to acknowledge that it makes sense for teachers to use a variety of approaches in their teaching that promote active thinking. Therefore, sometimes it is appropriate to use a direct style of teaching and at other times it is appropriate to get children 'doing things'. The key point to emphasise is that activities do not necessarily result in learning if they do not promote active thinking.

LEARNING BY DISCOVERY

The view that learners need to somehow 'discover' information for themselves is not supported by research evidence. According to Coe et al. (2014):

Enthusiasm for 'discovery learning' is not supported by research evidence, which broadly favours direct instruction . . . . Although learners do need to build new understanding on what they already know, if teachers want them to learn new ideas, knowledge or methods they need to teach them directly.

(p23)

However, that said, the skill of independent learning is an important skill for learners to master. Therefore, it is important to provide a balance between independent learning and direct instruction. It is also important to ensure that students do not develop misconceptions through independent learning.

PRAISE

The over-use of praise can create a culture of low expectations. According to Coe et al. (2014), *Praise for students may be seen as affirming and positive, but a number of studies suggest that the wrong kinds of praise can be very harmful to learning* (p22).

You can praise learners' efforts and their achievements, but the praise needs to be genuine and deserved. It is important to praise students when they have invested effort into something and also to praise their achievements when they are deserved, but it is also important not to communicate a message that students will receive praise for doing the minimum that is expected of them. The use of praise in classrooms should reinforce a culture of high expectations rather than transmitting the message that learners will receive praise regardless of their efforts or achievements.

LEARNING STYLES

The concept of grouping children into a dominant learning style has been discredited in the research community. According to Coe et al. (2014), *The psychological evidence is clear that there are no benefits for learning from trying to present information to learners in their preferred learning style* (p24).

There are benefits to incorporating opportunities for visual, auditory and kinaesthetic learning in classrooms. This ensures that learners can receive information through different channels. However, the idea that some learners are either visual learners, auditory learners or kinaesthetic learners is dangerous because an effective learner is able to learn using all channels. Grouping children into preferred learning styles closes down opportunities for learning rather than opening up opportunities for learning.

ABILITY GROUPING

The research on grouping arrangements in classrooms broadly favours mixed ability or flexible grouping arrangements. According to Coe et al. (2014), *Evidence on the effects of grouping by ability, either by allocating students to different classes, or to within-class groups, suggests that it makes very little difference to learning outcomes* (p23).

Although ability grouping might make it easier for the teacher to target the needs of specific groups of learners, it perpetuates the myth that learners within a group have exactly the same learning needs. Ability grouping also perpetuates a culture of low expectations because children placed into lower ability groups are often subjected to low teacher expectations and therefore they make less progress. In addition, in-class ability grouping results in elaborate and time-consuming differentiated activities or content, and this widens the ability gap. Instead, teachers need to consider how all learners can access the same content by providing specific support (adult support or other forms of scaffolding) to enable all learners to achieve the same learning outcomes where possible.

The problem with ability grouping is that learners are often placed in the same ability group for all subjects. In reality, they are often not 'high achievers' or 'low achievers' in all subjects. Additionally, their abilities within a subject can fluctuate; they may be strong in one aspect of a subject and weak in another aspect of that subject. Therefore, flexible grouping arrangements are more likely to be more responsive to learners' needs than keeping a student in a fixed ability group. Ability groups also perpetuate the myth that intelligence is static.

DEPLOYMENT OF TEACHING ASSISTANTS

Evidence suggests that the everyday deployment of teaching assistants (TAs) in classrooms is not leading to the desired effect of raising standards. According to Sharples et al. (2015):

> *The typical deployment and use of TAs, under everyday conditions, is not leading to improvements in academic outcomes ... pupils receiving the most support from TAs made less progress than similar pupils who received little or no support from TAs. There was also evidence that the negative impact was most marked for pupils with the highest levels of SEN.*

(p10)

It is vital that all learners receive their entitlement to be educated by a qualified teacher. It is important that teaching assistants develop independent learning skills in students and focus on promoting learning rather than task completion.

Teaching assistants need to make better use of questioning to promote learning and independent thinking so that learners do not become dependent on the TA (Sharples et al., 2015). The evidence suggests that TAs have a greater impact on learning when they deliver targeted interventions that they are trained to deliver rather than simply providing learners with general support in the classroom (Sharples et al., 2015).

CASE STUDY

A secondary school in Birmingham provided a professional development day for teachers and teaching assistants to work together and discuss effective practice. The professional development day was supported by a senior lecturer from a local university who was responsible for delivering the university's PGCert SENCO (Special Educational Needs Coordinator) qualification. Throughout the day, teachers and teaching assistants were able to explore their roles in relation to best practice and discuss approaches to supporting one another within a classroom setting. The senior lecturer provided case study material to support staff to understand examples of poor practice in relation to the deployment of teaching assistants. Teaching assistants were also given an opportunity to discuss the challenges they faced and teachers were asked to consider solutions to address these.

KEY RESEARCH

Key aspects of effective pedagogy are summarised below.

- *Spacing out learning: The same amount of time spent reviewing or practising leads to much greater long-term retention if it is spread out, with gaps in between to allow forgetting.*

- *Interleaving: Learning in a single block can create better immediate performance and higher confidence but interleaving with other tasks or topics leads to better long-term retention and transfer of skills.*

- *Varying the learning context, types of task or practice, rather than keeping them constant and predictable, improves later retention, even though it makes learning harder in the short term.*

(Coe et al., 2014, p17)

CASE STUDY

A primary school has developed a teaching and learning programme that provides teachers with an opportunity to choose their own areas of professional development within the context of the school's priorities. Teachers are able to work together on projects if they have chosen professional development areas that overlap or complement one another. The school has also partnered with a local university to enable teachers to work towards credits for related qualifications. The programme supports the school's priorities while providing teachers with a degree of autonomy and flexibility in relation to their own development. At the end of the programme, teachers are asked to deliver an introduction to their project and disseminate results among the staff. In one recent example, two colleagues worked together to strengthen their existing practice in relation to retrieval practice. The two teachers used social media to discuss and exchange ideas with other professionals and then they discussed their ideas before trialling them in the classroom. The teachers created a list of the strategies they had trialled and then shared these with colleagues to disseminate their findings.

PROFESSIONAL REFLECTION

Think carefully about your existing approach to space out learning, interleave and vary the learning context. Identify your strengths and areas for development and discuss these with a trusted colleague. Think about how effectively you blend these modes and methods, and how you can further develop or strengthen your existing practice.

NEXT STEPS

Identify how your existing practice supports teaching assistants to develop independent learning skills in learners. Think about your strengths and areas for development and identify how you can address these areas in your future practice.

TAKE 5

- Consider how you use praise in your classroom. How can you further develop your use of praise to reinforce a culture of high expectations?

- Identify the teaching methods that you use to promote active thinking. How often do you use these?

- Think carefully about how your teaching promotes learners' skills in relation to independence.

- Consider how you respond and adapt your teaching without unnecessarily elaborate or differentiated approaches.

- Think carefully about how you ensure that learners do not develop misconceptions through independent learning.

WHAT HAVE YOU LEARNED?

This chapter has addressed the key myths that are typically associated with Ofsted inspections. It has also addressed myths that relate to planning, teaching and assessment, as well as those that relate to the wider context of teaching and learning. Several common myths have also been addressed in relation to active learning, use of praise, deployment of teaching assistants and learning styles. Some case study material has also been presented to support your reflection and exemplify effective practice.

FURTHER READING

Barton, C and Bennett, T (2019) *The Researched Guide to Education Myths: An Evidence-informed Guide for Teachers*. Melton: John Catt.

Christodoulou, D (2014) *Seven Myths About Education*. Oxford: Routledge.

3

RESEARCH INTO THE QUALITY OF EDUCATION

WHAT WILL YOU LEARN?

This chapter introduces you to some key research in relation to the four areas of judgement within the Education Inspection Framework (Ofsted, 2019). National and international research is outlined to support your current understanding of curriculum and curriculum design, and we provide some opportunities for you to reflect on your current practice and provision. The chapter also outlines existing research on effective subject knowledge and pedagogy, and we present this within the context of the new framework and its requirements. Additionally, some practical guidance is provided in relation to the inspection process, and the effective and consistent implementation of behaviour management policies. This guidance draws on existing research that demonstrates the impact of bullying on learners and learners' attainment. The chapter then introduces the concept of resilience, and we emphasise the importance of relationships and belongingness within the context of positive school culture. The role of leadership and management is discussed, and some practical strategies are provided to exemplify and illuminate examples of best practice in relation to this aspect of the new framework.

QUALITY OF EDUCATION

What is taught, how it is taught (Biesta, 2009) and who is included in the curriculum (Young, 2013) are key principles that underpin effective curriculum design. Research suggests that the humanities subjects have been marginalised from the primary curriculum (Barnes and Scoffham, 2017; Ofsted, 2002). In addition, research indicates that learners in receipt of pupil premium are less likely to take

EBacc subjects compared with those not in receipt of pupil premium (Allen and Thompson, 2016).

International research demonstrates that curriculum narrowing is not specific to the United Kingdom. According to Berliner (2011), it has become commonplace across the United States in response to the pressures of high-stakes testing. In Australia, evidence suggests that testing regimes have led to a reduction in the time spent on non-assessed subjects and impacted detrimentally on classroom peda-gogy (Polesel et al., 2014) as a result of teaching to the test. Research suggests that teachers have been discouraged from experimenting with teaching strategies in the quest to improve test results (Ehren et al., 2015; Jones et al., 2017).

In response to these issues identified in research, the Education Inspection Framework focuses specifically on curriculum breadth in schools. In addition, it focuses sharply on how well learners are taught and the impact of teaching on out-comes for learners. There is a greater focus on effective pedagogy than in previous inspection frameworks, but what does this mean?

Evidence suggests that teacher subject knowledge has a strong impact on students' learning (Coe et al., 2014). This is a key component of effective pedagogy. Subject knowledge can be broken down into the following categories:

- *Content knowledge can be defined as teachers' knowledge of the subject they are teaching.*

- *Pedagogical knowledge is teachers' knowledge of effective teaching methods.*

- *Pedagogical content knowledge is teachers' knowledge of how to teach the particular subject or topic.*

(Ofsted, 2019)

Pedagogical content knowledge is consistently related to pupils' outcomes (Baumert et al., 2010; Wayne and Youngs, 2003). Baumert et al. (2010) found that teachers with greater content knowledge have higher levels of pedagogical content knowledge, which in itself leads to greater attention to cognitive activation in their teaching.

In addition to subject knowledge, research suggests that having the opportunity to learn correlates positively with attainment (Stallings, 1985; Muijs and Reynolds, 2003; Scheerens and Bosker, 1997). The opportunity to learn is influenced by the time spent on tasks and the amount of time that pupils are actively engaged in learning during the lesson (Ofsted, 2019). However, it is important to emphasise that active engagement in the process of learning does not just relate to the time that learners spend on completing tasks. It also relates to the time spent actively thinking about and processing the lesson content.

Assessment for learning is also a key component of effective pedagogy. Formative assessment has been found to have a significant positive effect on attainment (Black and Wiliam, 1998; Hattie, 2009; Siraj-Blatchford et al., 2002). Summarising learning at specific points during a lesson and making connections between different parts of a lesson or between learning in different lessons is important in promoting learning (Rosenshine and Stevens, 1986; Creemers and Kyriakides, 2008). Effective use of questioning within lessons enables learners to develop mastery of the subject content (Smith et al., 2004; Brophy and Good, 1986; Creemers, 1994). Effective questioning also enables teachers to check learners' understanding, identify and respond to misconceptions. It is likely that a combination of recall and higher order questions is effective in promoting learning (Ofsted, 2019).

The clarity of teacher explanations is a key component of effective pedagogy. Effective teachers can communicate clearly and directly with their learners, without going beyond their levels of comprehension (Smith and Land, 1981; Walberg, 1986; Muijs and Reynolds, 2003). Dual coding is the practice of representing information both visually and verbally, and is said to be effective in promoting understanding (Ofsted, 2019). Visual information in the form of diagrams, objects, pictures, videos and photographs can be used to support teachers in relaying verbal information.

Research suggests that in-class differentiation, through providing differentiated teaching, activities or resources, does not generally lead to gains in attainment (Hattie, 2009). However, adapting teaching in a responsive way – for example, by providing focused support to pupils who are working at lower stages of development within a subject to enable them to achieve the same learning outcomes as other pupils is likely to improve attainment (Deunk et al., 2018).

Effective sequencing of lessons and use of retrieval practice helps learners to remember content. Research also suggests that repeating and reviewing key concepts (Scheerens and Bosker, 1997; Seidel and Shavelson, 2007) is a key characteristic of effective teaching. As Sweller (2011) has pointed out, *if nothing in the long-term memory has been altered, nothing has been learned*. An effective approach to curriculum planning is to block learning and repeat practice over time, as this leads to better long-term retention of knowledge (Rawson and Kintsch, 2005). There is increasing evidence that interleaving can improve long-term retention (Richland et al., 2005; Rohrer et al., 2015). Interleaving is the sequencing of learning tasks so that similar content or tasks are interspersed with different types of content or task rather than being consecutive. This results in a more variable and challenging learning experience, but leads to better long-term retention.

Retrieval practice strengthens memory and aids long-term retention (Barenberg et al., 2018; Roediger and Karpicke, 2006).

The Education Inspection Framework (2019) emphasises that schools should ensure that *a rigorous approach to the teaching of reading develops learners' confidence and enjoyment in reading. At the early stages of learning to read, reading materials are closely matched to learners' phonics knowledge* (p10). Research suggests that effective evidence-based reading instruction has five essential components: phonemic awareness, phonics, fluency, vocabulary and comprehension, all of which matter, provided phonemic awareness and decoding skills are acquired as an essential precondition (Buckingham et al., 2013). Schools therefore need to ensure that the skill of decoding for accurate word recognition is established as a prerequisite skill for developing fluency and reading for understanding. Schools need to ensure that learners in higher Key Stages who have not mastered the skill of word recognition are provided with phonics intervention to enable them to make progress in their reading development.

BEHAVIOUR AND ATTITUDES

Research demonstrates that bullying can have a negative impact on pupil attainment, and that reducing bullying is associated with improved attainment (Brown and Taylor, 2008; Fonagy et al., 2005). Schools should take steps to eradicate all forms of bullying and incidents need to be addressed in accordance with the school policy. The school behaviour management policy should be effective and consistently implemented by all teachers. Inspectors will focus on students' attitudes to learning within lessons. This will include aspects such as their punctuality and participation in lessons.

PERSONAL DEVELOPMENT

The school curriculum should promote resilience. Resilience develops through interaction between the person and the environment (Beltman et al., 2011). Students are more likely to be resilient if they learn in a positive environment and develop effective relationships with their peers and teachers. Fostering a sense of belonging is also important. Shochet et al. (2006) found a significant relationship between adolescents' feelings of belonging in school and their mental health. This can be achieved by developing a positive school culture that promotes respect for all members of the school community and that values diversity. Learners will need access to a mental health curriculum that teaches the skills of emotional and social regulation, as well as developing their mental health literacy.

In addition, from September 2020 all primary schools will be required to teach inclusive relationships education and secondary schools will be required to teach inclusive relationships and sex education.

CASE STUDY

A secondary school introduced a mental health curriculum to all students in Year 8. The students were taught about mental health and specific mental health conditions, including anxiety, stress, depression and self-harm. In addition, they had sessions on the relationship between social media and mental health. They were introduced to strategies for managing their own emotions, including emotional regulation strategies. The programme included guest speakers from the local community who came into school and led presentations on how they had managed their own mental health. One of these sessions was led by a local rugby player who had experienced poor mental health. The students completed a mental health literacy questionnaire before and after the intervention to ascertain their own knowledge of mental health. There was an increase in students' mental health literacy scores and, more importantly, by the end of the intervention students knew some strategies for managing their own mental health and they knew where to go to access support and advice.

LEADERSHIP AND MANAGEMENT

Inspectors will evaluate the effectiveness of leadership and management in the school. Research demonstrates that leadership is the most important factor in school effectiveness (Reynolds et al., 2014). However, approaches to effective leadership are dependent on school context and phase (Day et al., 2010).

Effective leaders provide staff with access to high-quality professional development opportunities. Cordingley et al. (2015) identified the following features of effective professional development. These are summarised below.

- Longer programmes tend to be more effective than short-term interventions, and most effective professional development has to last at least two terms to have an impact.

- Effective professional development requires follow-up, practice and support.

- Professional development needs to be relevant to the everyday work of teachers.

- Professional development needs to be differentiated by teachers' starting points and should not just have a one-size-fits-all approach.

Effective leaders also promote effective parental engagement. Research demonstrates an association between parental engagement and children's learning (Desforges, 2003; Higgins and Katsipataki, 2015). This can be achieved through developing clear and transparent communication with parents, adopting a consultative approach, involving parents in various aspects of school life, seeking and acting on parental feedback, and through developing parental workshops on curriculum themes and aspects of personal development. These opportunities provide parents with knowledge and skills so that they can more effectively support their child's education.

CASE STUDY

A primary school had previously adopted the strategy of differentiation during lessons. Learning tasks were differentiated three ways. A challenging task was set for the children who were working at a higher stage of development. An age-appropriate task was set for the 'middle' group and a basic task was set for children who were identified as having special educational needs and disabilities.

The teachers noticed that the children who were working at lower stages of development were falling further behind their peers. The ability gap was widening rather than narrowing. In addition, the children in the lower two groups were not exposed to the higher level learning challenges that the more able learners were asked to complete.

The leadership team decided to cease the practice of differentiation in most lessons. All groups were set the same task so that they all had the opportunity to achieve the same learning outcomes. Additional support, resources and scaffolding were provided to the children working at lower stages of development to enable them to achieve the learning outcomes. A range of graduated challenge tasks was provided for children who had completed the main task and required an additional challenge in the lesson. Challenge tasks were placed in green, amber and red baskets, and children were allowed to choose the level of challenge that they felt comfortable with.

Very quickly all groups started to make greater progress and the ability gap began to narrow.

PROFESSIONAL REFLECTION

Reflect on the professional development opportunities that are currently offered within your setting or context. Think about how you ensure follow-up, practice and support in relation to these opportunities and identify areas for development. How are these opportunities differentiated to recognise teachers' needs and starting points? How can the existing programme be refined or strengthened to better reflect these needs? Discuss your ideas with a trusted colleague.

NEXT STEPS

Think about how your setting promotes effective parental engagement. Make a list of the opportunities that are provided for parents to engage with the school. Identify the different aspects of school life that they support. What are the areas for development that need to be prioritised to further improve existing levels of parental engagement?

TAKE 5

- Think carefully about the school behaviour policy and how consistently it is used and applied by all teachers. Identify how this consistency can be further improved.

- Reflect on how your professional development opportunities enable teachers to develop their subject knowledge.

- Plan opportunities for your professional development programmes to support teachers' understanding of effective pedagogy in relation to sequencing.

- Identify how the curriculum offer supports the development of learners' resilience. Plan opportunities to further strengthen this offer.

- Think carefully about your school culture. How does it value diversity and promote respect? Identify your strengths and areas for development.

WHAT HAVE YOU LEARNED?

This chapter has introduced you to some key research in relation to the four areas of judgement within the Education Inspection Framework. National and international research has been outlined to support your current understanding of curriculum and curriculum design, and we have provided some opportunities for you to reflect on your current practice and provision. The chapter has also outlined existing research on effective subject knowledge and pedagogy, and we have presented this within the context of the new framework and its requirements. Additionally, some practical guidance has been provided in relation to the inspection process, and the effective and consistent implementation of behaviour management policies. This guidance has drawn on existing research that has demonstrated the impact of bullying on learners and learners' attainment. The chapter then introduced the concept of resilience, and we have emphasised the importance of relationships and belongingness within the context of positive school culture.

The role of leadership and management has been discussed, and some practical strategies have been provided to exemplify and illuminate examples of best practice in relation to this aspect of the new framework.

FURTHER READING

Hughes, D (2019) *Future-proof Your School: Steering Culture, Driving School Improvement, Developing Excellence*. St Albans: Critical Publishing.

Shute, R and Slee, P (2016) *Mental Health and Wellbeing through Schools*. Oxford: Routledge.

4

THE FRAMEWORK: QUALITY OF EDUCATION

WHAT WILL YOU LEARN?

This chapter explores the quality of education within the context of the Education Inspection Framework (Ofsted, 2019). It introduces and discusses intent, implementation and impact as the three aspects of the quality of education and discusses the implications of each for school leadership teams and teachers. Within intent, the chapter emphasises the importance of providing learners with an ambitious curriculum that develops cultural capital and discussion is provided to demonstrate effective practice. Practical guidance is also offered in relation to curriculum breadth, and to the planning and sequencing of a curriculum. The chapter then moves to implementation and in doing so emphasises the importance of teachers having good and secure subject knowledge. It also outlines the value of modelling as a method to present and impart this knowledge. Some practical strategies are then provided to support you in helping your learners to remember content, and we emphasise the importance of assessment and reading as cornerstones of an effective curriculum. The chapter then introduces the third aspect of the quality of education before moving on to provide some research and case study material to encourage your reflection on current professional practice.

KEY POLICY

The Education Inspection Framework places more emphasis on the quality of education that learners receive in comparison with previous inspection frameworks. The focus in this strand of the framework is on the quality of the curriculum. The framework evaluates the following aspects of the quality of education.

INTENT
The quality of the planned curriculum

IMPLEMENTATION
The quality of teaching

IMPACT
The outcomes achieved by learners

- Intent: this relates to the quality of the planned curriculum.

- Implementation: this relates to the quality of teaching.

- Impact: this relates to the outcomes achieved by learners.

Each of these aspects is now discussed to support you in understanding how to address them.

INTENT

Intent focuses on the following aspects.

- *Leaders take on or construct a curriculum that is ambitious and designed to give all learners, particularly the most disadvantaged and those with special educational needs and/or disabilities (SEND) or high needs the knowledge and cultural capital they need to succeed in life;*

- *the provider's curriculum is coherently planned and sequenced towards cumulatively sufficient knowledge and skills for future learning and employment;*

- *the provider has the same academic, technical or vocational ambitions for almost all learners. Where this is not practical – for example, for some learners with high levels of SEND – its curriculum is designed to be ambitious and to meet their needs;*

- *learners study the full curriculum. Providers ensure this by teaching a full range of subjects for as long as possible, 'specialising' only when necessary.*

(Ofsted, 2019, p9)

AN AMBITIOUS CURRICULUM

There is a clear expectation in the Education Inspection Framework that schools will provide learners with a curriculum that is ambitious. The term 'ambitious' is not defined in the framework, but state schools in England are required by law to teach the National Curriculum (DfE, 2013) which states:

> *The National Curriculum provides pupils with an introduction to the essential knowledge they need to be educated citizens. It introduces pupils to the best that has been thought and said, and helps engender an appreciation of human creativity and achievement.*

(DfE, 2013)

The National Curriculum therefore provides a foundation for schools to plan a tailored curriculum that meets the needs of learners and the communities that schools serve. The curriculum is the heart of the Education Inspection Framework (Ofsted, 2019). Inspectors will evaluate the extent to which the curriculum engages and motivates learners, and its effectiveness in providing learners with essential knowledge, skills and attitudes that they will need in the future.

The curriculum should be designed so that it is exciting and maintains learners' interest. It should be relevant and contemporary, and address current societal issues. Examples of important themes include climate change and environmental sustainability, mental health, discrimination and prejudice, and politics. The curriculum should provide learners with the knowledge and skills they will need for future employment. In addition, it should develop their confidence so that learners can perform at their best. The curriculum should be sufficiently ambitious and challenging so that learners can operate at the limits of their capabilities. It should be designed to ensure that learners are mentally active. It should capture learners' interests, motivation and fascination through opportunities for deep, focused meaningful learning. It should develop within learners' positive character attributes that include resilience, emotional and social regulation, persistence, integrity, empathy, and a commitment to social justice and inclusion. The curriculum should embed creativity and provide learners with rich exploration opportunities for making memories. It should foster a sense of awe and wonder, and enable learners to step out of their comfort zones. It should provide learners with cultural capital to 'future proof' them. A rich and stimulating curriculum allows learners to be scientists, artists, designers, geographers, historians, authors or poets. It provides learners with rich, active learning experiences through which they learn using their senses. It should inspire learners to want to study subjects more deeply and at a higher level, thus fostering a love of specific subjects. It should enable learners to make connections between different subjects so that learners begin to recognise that skills and knowledge in one subject can be applied in other subjects. Learning through the outdoors, educational visits and guest speakers, and learning through exploration and investigation, as opposed to learning through PowerPoint presentations, are useful strategies to spark interest, motivation and curiosity.

CULTURAL CAPITAL

Pierre Bourdieu (1930–2002) was interested in how cultural capital is a source of inequality. Cultural capital has traditionally been associated with social class. The more cultural capital a person possesses, the greater chance they have of achieving social mobility. According to Bourdieu, cultural capital exists in three forms: embodied, objectified and institutional. An example of embodied cultural capital is accent. One's accent can restrict or support their chances of achieving social mobility. In addition, the more advanced one's vocabulary, the greater a person's chances of achieving social mobility. Objectified cultural capital is demonstrated through possessions because cultural capital can be exchanged for economic capital. People with greater cultural capital are more likely to live in bigger houses, wear designer clothes and purchase expensive cars. Institutional cultural capital is related to the type of school someone attends or their qualifications. Someone with a degree possesses more cultural capital than someone without a degree, and someone with a postgraduate degree holds more cultural capital than someone with an undergraduate degree. Someone who attends an independent school holds more cultural capital than someone who attends a state school. These forms of cultural capital can be exchanged for economic capital. Broadly, cultural capital is the accumulation of knowledge, attitudes and skills that enable an individual to demonstrate their cultural competence and social status. Cultural capital can therefore be demonstrated through social interests – for example, people with greater cultural capital may visit art galleries, museums, the opera and theatre.

So, how does this relate to the school curriculum? Given that cultural capital can be a major source of inequality, the curriculum should be designed to provide all learners with cultural capital so that they can access future opportunities. There is no justifiable reason why people from working-class backgrounds cannot access high-status jobs. However, professions including law and politics are dominated by those from middle- and upper-class backgrounds. There is no justifiable reason why people from working-class backgrounds cannot access the top universities. The stark reality is that working-class people are significantly under-represented in high-status and high-earning professions, and restricted from accessing the top universities. Sadly, discrimination and prejudice operate within our society; the capacity to purchase education provides greater future educational and employment opportunities, regardless of intelligence, and individuals continue to be judged on the basis of their accent, breadth of vocabulary and their cultural experiences. Through embedding cultural capital in the curriculum, it is possible to increase learners' cultural capital by providing them with opportunities and experiences that they would not normally gain access to because of their social status and background. It is a way of providing all students with equality of opportunity so that learners from all backgrounds can achieve their full potential.

So, what are the implications for curriculum planning? One way of increasing learners' cultural capital is to develop their vocabulary. Increasing not only the number of words that learners know, understand and use in their communication, but also the complexity of the vocabulary is one way of providing them with more cultural capital. Identify the complex vocabulary that relates to the subject matter that you are teaching and insist that learners use this vocabulary in both oral and written communication. Planning educational visits to places of interest is another way of developing cultural capital. Some learners may never have opportunities to leave their immediate locality, and visits to museums, historical sites, businesses, theatres and contrasting localities provide learners with rich experiences that broaden their interests and ambitions. Visits to local universities may provide learners with opportunities to be taught by leading experts within a subject and also raise their future aspirations. Bringing leading experts from the world of sport, business, the arts, sciences and humanities into the classroom to lead workshops can be aspirational for many young people. Bringing theatre groups, authors, poets, artists and designers into school can provide learners with opportunities to learn from people who make their livings within the professions.

The above suggestions are not exhaustive. They are intended to spark your thinking about how you can develop cultural capital within your subject area. Social deprivation does not have to be a barrier to success, but to succeed learners will require various forms of cultural capital so that they can perform when they write applications for university places and jobs, and attend interviews. It is sad that people are judged on the basis of their cultural capital rather than on their ability, but ensuring that all learners have the same opportunities for developing cultural capital is an attempt to level the playing field.

PLANNING AND SEQUENCING THE CURRICULUM

Inspectors are interested in how you plan and sequence the curriculum. In primary schools, the starting point for planning is often the activities that children will undertake. Teachers are often assigned a topic or theme and they immediately start thinking of activities that children can do. The problem with this approach is that the knowledge and skills that children need to acquire often become an afterthought. The attention is often on the experiences that children will be provided with.

Although it is important to provide learners with a wide variety of stimulating experiences, it is essential to consider first and foremost what knowledge and skills you want the children to learn. What do you want them to know and be able to do by the end of this unit of work? There is little value in children making Roman mosaics and Roman shields if they do not know key facts about the Romans. These might include knowledge of the chronology related to that period, knowledge of the key events that occurred during the period, knowledge of the significant individuals who lived during that time, knowledge of important people and their lives and knowledge of key vocabulary. So, the starting point for your planning needs to be focused on the knowledge and skills that you want your learners to develop.

You then need to decide how to sequence the knowledge and skills across a unit of work. Some teachers find it helpful to work backwards. If you know what you want your learners to know and be able to do by the end of the unit, you can then work backwards from this point to identify how the knowledge and skills will be sequentially ordered through the unit of work. Essentially, you will need to make decisions within a unit of work about what to teach first and the order of subsequent learning. You will need to consider carefully at the planning stage how the knowledge and skills will progress through the unit. It is important to share the bigger picture with your learners so that they know how each of the stages within a topic are supporting them to achieve a final goal.

If you know what the final outcome in a unit of work is, then you should be able to identify all the aspects of knowledge and skills (components) that will be required for learners to achieve this outcome. These components can then be taught throughout the unit of work and arranged in a logical sequence that enables learners to progressively develop their knowledge, skills and understanding.

A clear and well-sequenced unit of work will support you to identify the next steps in learning. This will enable you to provide specific students with additional levels of challenge, particularly the more able students who can progress more quickly through the sequence of learning. A well-sequenced unit plan will also enable you to take the learning back a stage for learners who require additional consolidation.

CURRICULUM BREADTH

In recent years, there has been a narrowing of the curriculum, particularly in primary schools where mathematics and English have been prioritised over other subjects. This has led to the marginalisation of the foundation subjects and therefore lack of curriculum breadth. However, a broad curriculum in both primary and secondary schools is essential. Not only does a broad curriculum engage learners and support them in experiencing success in the subjects that they are more confident in, it prepares them well for future employment. Young people will need a wide variety of skills in the future for employment. They will need to be creative, adaptable, and possess broad knowledge and skills. They will need to have good interpersonal skills, be able to work in teams, be resilient and able to solve problems. A broad and rich curriculum should provide children with all of these skills. It should motivate them, inspire them and enable them to recognise their own strengths, talents and interests. Curriculum breadth promotes confidence and a positive sense of self. It maintains children's motivation and interest.

It is important that children have opportunities to study subjects in-depth rather than studying them superficially. An effective curriculum plan should enable learners to develop subject-specific knowledge and skills through high-quality teaching and opportunities for exploration and investigation.

In addition, schools should aim to develop curriculum breadth through a range of stimulating extra-curricular activities. The extra-curricular offer should provide opportunities for learners to specialise in a broad range of subjects. The introduction of a student debating society, for example, can provide learners with cultural capital.

IMPLEMENTATION

The Education Inspection Framework will evaluate the extent to which:

- *teachers have good knowledge of the subject(s) and courses they teach;*

- *teachers present subject matter clearly, promoting appropriate discussion about the subject matter they are teaching;*

- *teaching is designed to help learners to remember in the long term the content they have been taught and to integrate new knowledge into larger concepts;*

- *teachers and leaders use assessment well, for example to help learners embed and use knowledge fluently or to check understanding and inform teaching;*

- *teachers create an environment that allows the learner to focus on learning;*

- *a rigorous approach to the teaching of reading develops learners' confidence and enjoyment in reading.*

(Ofsted, 2019, pp9–10)

SUBJECT KNOWLEDGE

Good subject knowledge is essential for effective teaching. You need to ensure that you understand the subject matter and are able to explain it clearly to your learners. You also need to be aware of the misconceptions that learners may develop. During the process of planning lessons, it is advisable to research the possible misconceptions that learners may develop so that you can explicitly turn these into teaching points during the lesson. If you feel that your subject knowledge is insecure, you should research the content thoroughly prior to teaching it and talk to more experienced teachers in the school. You should also make sure that you are teaching age-appropriate content from the National Curriculum and content that is relevant to examination specifications in secondary schools. This will ensure that you pitch your lessons at an appropriately challenging level.

PRESENTING SUBJECT CONTENT

You will almost certainly need to use modelling in your lessons to show your learners what is expected. Modelling is the visual presentation of the subject content. You can model on the board a specific skill or aspect of knowledge that you want your learners to develop or you could model using a visualiser. You can also model the expectations of a specific task. The purpose of modelling is to demonstrate to learners what is expected of them. Modelling should be used in conjunction with verbal explanations of the subject content because verbal explanations on their own are usually less effective. Learners cannot always simply process auditory information. Many learners need to see the steps of learning being outlined.

You will need to consider carefully how to sequence the lesson content throughout the lesson to ensure that learners remain motivated and make progress. Consider breaking the lesson down into a series of smaller stages or chunks. When the learners have completed one task, you can model a second task which they then complete, which advances their learning further. This process can then be repeated. You probably will not want to structure all lessons like this. In some lessons, learners need to work on one task so that they achieve depth of learning. However, modelling should be an essential feature of most lessons.

You might wish to consider using photographs, objects, stories or videos to make the subject content more engaging. You might also wish to consider structuring lessons or units of work using Bloom's taxonomy or solo taxonomy. These are discussed in the research boxes below.

HELPING LEARNERS TO REMEMBER CONTENT

Once you have identified the knowledge and skills that you want your learners to know and be able to do, you need to consider how to help your learners to remember the subject content that you are teaching. You will need to revisit key content throughout the unit. Learners often need to be exposed to content several times before they retain it. The following strategies will support you in helping your learners to remember content.

- Do a short quiz at the start of each lesson to check their understanding of the previous lesson.

- Design an assessment task to assess knowledge and skills half-way through the unit.

- Design an assessment task to be used at the end of the unit.

- Provide learners with a summary of the key content they need to remember at the start of a unit.

- Do a quiz at the end of the lesson to check their understanding of the content.

- Provide your learners with worked examples and good models on a working wall.

- Develop a mnemonic to help them remember something.

USING ASSESSMENT WELL

Assessment for learning is assessment that promotes learning, and informs planning and teaching. It is usually informal and takes place within and between lessons. Examples include:

- checking on understanding of prior learning at the start of a lesson through the use of a short assessment task;

- introducing an assessment task immediately after you have modelled the new learning to check understanding;

- noticing and responding to misconceptions within the lesson so that learners make greater progress;

- adapting the lesson in response to learners' needs during the lesson;

- marking work with learners in the lesson and talking to them about their learning;

- using questioning and short quizzes during lessons to check understanding;

- marking work and addressing common misconceptions with the learners in the next lesson;

- providing learners with feedback on their work and building in time for them to respond to the feedback in the next lesson;

- using the plenary to check learners' understanding of the lesson content;

- using self-assessment and peer-assessment during the lesson.

It is not necessary to use all of these strategies in a single lesson. In addition, regular summative assessments which take place at fixed points in time across the year can be utilised to inform planning and teaching, particularly if topics are being revisited. These assessment tasks enable you to identify misconceptions and you can address these when the topic is next taught. In this way, summative assessment can be used formatively to inform planning and teaching.

CREATING AN EFFECTIVE LEARNING ENVIRONMENT

It is important to create a calm working atmosphere that is free from distractions. You therefore need to make your expectations clear from the start. Standing at the door to greet learners as they enter the room creates an orderly entry to the room. Providing them with a task to complete as soon as they sit down ensures that they quickly settle down and get straight into learning. Provide learners with clear rules for behaviour when you are teaching the class. Ensure that your expectations in relation to acceptable noise levels are made explicit so that learners know what your expectations are. Reward good behaviour and use sanctions when behaviour starts to interrupt learning. Aim to create a calm working atmosphere in the classroom. Be consistent and if you say that you are going to do something, then make sure that you do it.

TEACHING READING

The new framework includes a reading 'deep dive' in primary, junior, infant and lower middle school settings (Ofsted, 2019). In these settings, the deep dive is a mandatory part of the inspection process under the new framework. It is essential that all children learn to read fluently and that they do so as quickly as possible. This is because children with higher levels of fluency are able to learn more quickly, and can therefore read and gain knowledge for themselves. In other settings, the inspection process will still examine the extent to which there is a rigorous approach to the teaching of reading, and how this develops learners' confidence and enjoyment in reading. In the early years and in Key Stage 1, there must be a systematic approach to the teaching of synthetic phonics. Schools must be able to demonstrate how the phonics scheme ensures progression in children's phonic knowledge, and that reading books are accurately matched to the phonics content that children have been taught. Lessons should be clearly structured to ensure that children develop their phonic knowledge and their skill in blending phonemes for reading and segmenting words into their constituent phonemes for spelling. In addition, teachers must ensure that children apply their phonic knowledge in their reading and writing, and have opportunities to revisit the alphabetic code. Teachers should also provide children with access to real books so that they develop an enjoyment of reading. The teaching of phonics is time limited and ensures accurate word reading skills. However, as children progress in their reading development, inspectors will be interested in children's comprehension of texts and their skills in retrieval, deduction and inference. Inspectors will be interested in phonics provision for children in Key Stages 2 and 3 who have not mastered the skill of word reading.

Reading brings clear benefits to learners and is an important aspect of the new framework. It is crucial that teachers and leaders in all settings take action to build a culture of reading for enjoyment. Reading must not be seen as the responsibility of a single practitioner or department. All teachers and classroom-based staff have a responsibility to promote and foster learners' confidence and enjoyment in reading. All teachers are teachers of reading, which should be integrated into most lessons. This can be done in many ways and examples include:

- dedicated class reading time can be used to provide protected time for reading activities;
- providing opportunities for children to engage with well-known or celebrated authors in their field of study;
- incorporating specific reading activities in existing curriculum planning documents;
- parental involvement to support reading activities beyond the school context;
- book donation schemes that enable the exchange of reading material between adults and children;
- active promotion of World Book Day and national and international reading events;
- providing welcoming and accessible spaces that are dedicated to reading.

CASE STUDY

A primary school purchased some resources to support the teaching of synthetic phonics. However, it became apparent that many of the children in the Reception class were not ready to learn phonics. Many had poor language skills and their skills in visual discrimination, visual memory and auditory discrimination were significantly below age-related expectations. These factors impacted detrimentally on the children's readiness to learn phonics.

The practitioner developed a programme to support the development of children's visual and auditory skills. The teacher recognised that visual and auditory discrimination, and visual and auditory sequencing and mentor skills are critical for children's subsequent development in phonics. The activities included:

- recognising odd-one-out activity using objects, photographs, line drawings and silhouettes;
- sorting and matching activities using shapes and other objects;
- memory games;

- activities to support the development of fine motor skills, including threading beads and scrunching paper;

- activities to develop auditory discrimination, including taking children on sound walks in the outdoor environment.

After several weeks of completing these activities, the children had the prerequisite skills that they needed to start learning phonics.

IMPACT

The Education Inspection Framework states:

- *learners develop detailed knowledge and skills across the curriculum and, as a result, achieve well. Where relevant, this is reflected in results from national tests and examinations that meet government expectations, or in the qualifications obtained;*

- *learners are ready for the next stage of education, employment or training. Where relevant, they gain qualifications that allow them to go on to destinations that meet their interests, aspirations and the intention of their course of study. They read widely and often, with fluency and comprehension.*

(Ofsted, 2019, p10)

The impact of the curriculum can be evaluated through the gains that learners make in their knowledge, skills and attitudes. The impact of the curriculum can also be measured through the results that learners achieve in national tests and examinations. However, results are not the only measure of a successful curriculum. Impact can also be measured through learners' enjoyment of a subject and their motivation to read more about the subject independently. Igniting a passion for a subject is a real measure of impact. If the curriculum fosters a love of a subject, a desire to learn it deeply and motivation to continue studying it, then this is evidence of genuine and meaningful impact.

KEY RESEARCH

According to Coe et al. (2014):

The most effective teachers have deep knowledge of the subjects they teach, and when teachers' knowledge falls below a certain level it is a significant impediment to students' learning. As well as a strong understanding of the material being taught, teachers must also understand the ways students think about the content, be able to evaluate the thinking behind students' own methods and identify students' common misconceptions.

[Quality of Instruction] Includes elements such as effective questioning and use of assessment by teachers. Specific practices, like reviewing previous learning, providing model responses for students, giving adequate time for practice to embed skills securely Executive Summary 3 and progressively introducing new learning (scaffolding) are also elements of high-quality instruction.

(pp. 2-3)

CASE STUDY

A secondary school identified several students in Year 7 who had under-developed reading skills. These learners were assessed in their phonic knowledge, word recognition skills and reading comprehension skills. An intervention programme was designed to support the development of these skills and the students were taught to develop skills, including fluency and inference. The gaps in their phonic knowledge were also addressed in the intervention. After a term, the students made substantial progress in both their skills in work recognition and language comprehension.

PROFESSIONAL REFLECTION

Reflect on the subject(s) that you teach and identify opportunities for developing cultural capital and reading within specific units of work.

NEXT STEPS

Consider and reflect on your current understanding of the three aspects of the quality of education. Identify your strengths and areas for development in relation to the new framework and your learners' needs. Discuss these with colleagues in school and agree action points which you need to further develop.

TAKE 5

- Provide your learners with a broad, rich and stimulating curriculum.
- Plan for how you can develop learners' cultural capital within specific subjects.

(Continued)

(Continued)

- Plan opportunities for developing reading in all subjects.

- Identify potential misconceptions at the planning stage and address these in your teaching so that learners do not develop them.

- Plan opportunities for learners to learn through investigation and exploration.

WHAT HAVE YOU LEARNED?

This chapter has explored the quality of education within the context of the Education Inspection Framework. It has introduced and discussed intent, implementation and impact as the three aspects of the quality of education, and it has discussed the implications of each for both school leadership teams and teachers. The chapter has emphasised the importance of providing learners with an ambitious curriculum that develops cultural capital, and discussion has been provided to demonstrate effective practice. Practical guidance has also been offered in relation to curriculum breadth, and to the planning and sequencing of a curriculum. The chapter then moved on to implementation and in doing so has emphasised the importance of teachers having good and secure subject knowledge. It then argued the value of modelling as a method to present and impart this knowledge. Some practical strategies were then provided to support you in helping your learners to remember content and we emphasised the importance of assessment and reading as cornerstones of an effective curriculum. The chapter then introduced the third aspect of the quality of education before moving on to provide some research and case study material, which we hope has encouraged your critical reflection on current professional practice.

FURTHER READING

Horton, S, Beattie, L and Lannie, S (2018) *Reading at Greater Depth in Key Stage 2*. London: Learning Matters.

Quigley, A (2018) *Closing the Vocabulary Gap*. London: Routledge.

5

THE FRAMEWORK: BEHAVIOUR AND ATTITUDES

WHAT WILL YOU LEARN?

This chapter provides advice on how to manage learners' behaviour in lessons and how to promote good behaviour for learning. Many trainee teachers (and qualified teachers) have sleepless nights where they worry about learners' behaviour. It is easy to interpret negative behaviour as a personal response to you. However, this is rarely the case. Sadly, some young people have adverse childhood experiences, and these may affect their behaviour in school. Some may have developed a poor sense of self and this can detrimentally impact on their behaviour. Although poor behaviour is draining, it is important that you try to understand its root causes. Sanctions provide a 'quick fix' but they do not address the causes. This chapter outlines some important strategies that will support you in managing children's behaviour. The chapter also discusses the importance of establishing high expectations and some practical guidance is provided in relation to developing relationships and positive attitudes to learning. It also demonstrates the importance of establishing and embedding consistent rules and routines, and some case studies will be used to demonstrate some examples of effective practice in relation to classroom management. In this chapter you are encouraged to reflect on your current practice, and identify strengths and areas for development.

KEY POLICY

The Education Inspection Framework (Ofsted, 2019) states that inspectors will make a judgement on behaviour and attitudes by evaluating the extent to which:

- *the school has high expectations for learners' behaviour and conduct, and applies these expectations consistently and fairly. This is reflected in learners' behaviour and conduct;*

- *learners' attitudes to their education or training are positive. They are committed to their learning, know how to study effectively and do so, are resilient to setbacks and take pride in their achievements;*

- *learners have high attendance and are punctual;*

- *relationships among learners and staff reflect a positive and respectful culture. Leaders, teachers and learners create an environment where bullying, peer-on-peer abuse or discrimination are not tolerated. If they do occur, staff deal with issues quickly and effectively, and do not allow them to spread.*

(pp10–11)

ESTABLISHING EXPECTATIONS

Inspectors will check your expectations of learners' behaviour in lessons. Establishing high expectations for behaviour will minimise disruption and maximise time for learning for everyone. You will need to work hard with classes initially to ensure that you consistently reinforce your expectations. High expectations may include the following:

- ensuring that learners enter the classroom in an orderly manner by greeting them on the door;

- insisting that they work in silence at specific times when you ask them to work independently;

- ensuring that they are looking at you and listening to you when you are speaking to them – 'books closed, pens down, look this way';

- insisting that they persevere with tasks that they find difficult;

- establishing clear rules about movement around the room and sticking to a seating plan;

- setting clear expectations about participation in group work;

- being clear about how much work you expect them to complete in a specific time;

- managing transitions effectively as learners move from one activity to the next;

- establishing a reasonable working noise level;

- ensuring that learners attend lessons punctually;

- ensuring that learners bring the correct equipment with them to lessons.

YOUR LEARNERS NEED TO KNOW THAT . . .

YOU **CARE** FOR THEM AS PEOPLE AS WELL AS CARING FOR THEIR LEARNING

YOU **UNDERSTAND** THEM

YOU **BELIEVE** IN THEM

YOU **WILL FORGIVE** THEM WHEN THEY GET THINGS WRONG

DEVELOPING POSITIVE ATTITUDES TO LEARNING

Inspectors will look closely at attitudes to learning in lessons. They will look at whether learners are interested, motivated and engaged in their learning. They will evaluate the extent to which they listen carefully, persevere, ask questions, challenge each other respectfully, take ownership of their learning and work independently. These positive characteristics may need to be taught and consistently reinforced during lessons.

DEVELOPING POSITIVE RELATIONSHIPS

Establishing positive relationships with learners is the starting point to support you in developing good behaviour management. While this will not necessarily guarantee good behaviour, it will reduce the likelihood of negative behaviour occurring. Learners generally do not learn from teachers that they do not like. Your learners need to know that:

- you care for them as people as well as caring for their learning;

- you understand them;

- you believe in them;

- you will forgive them when they get things wrong.

Although you will need to establish clear behavioural expectations in every lesson, learners generally enjoy lessons if they like the teacher. Learners tend not to like teachers who shout, and it is often true that a noisy teacher produces a noisy class. Try not to shout unless necessary, and deal with issues firmly but calmly. It is easier to start firmly and then subsequently relax with a class. All learners will test you at first, so a 'no-nonsense' approach is best adopted. You should find that when learners are clear about your behavioural expectations you will then be able to relax with them and demonstrate a sense of humour as time progresses. Simple and effective ways of establishing relationships with new classes include the following:

- learn the names of all learners very quickly; a seating plan will help with this;

- smile;

- try to get to know your learners, including their interests outside of school;

- thank them for their contributions in class;

- acknowledge the effort they make with their work;

- create a 'can-do' culture so that learners start to believe in their abilities;

- apologise to learners if you make a mistake;

- tell them a little about yourself;

- be enthusiastic about your teaching; if you are excited, it will be infectious;

- use eye-contact;

- use their names in class.

RULES AND ROUTINES

Establishing clear expectations for learners' behaviour is critical, and it is important that you follow the whole-school policy in relation to rules and routines. Simple strategies such as greeting the learners as they enter the classroom sets the correct tone for the rest of the lesson. Displaying a task on the board for them to do as soon as they sit down ensures that there is no wasted learning time and this will minimise disruption. Establish clear expectations about punctuality to lessons and implement sanctions if learners turn up to lessons late. Read the school behaviour policy and ensure that you are familiar with the rules and routines of the school. If these are consistently applied by all teachers, learners clearly understand what is expected of them. Establish basic expectations. These include the following:

- when you talk, they must listen;

- mobile phones must be turned off and kept in their bags;

- insist that they listen carefully when other learners are answering questions or making other contributions to the lessons;

- insist that they value everyone's contribution;

- establish a zero-tolerance policy on the use of bad language in class and implement sanctions where necessary;

- develop clear rules on whether movement around the classroom is permitted;

- develop clear routines and expectations at the end of lessons – for example, tidying away, pushing chairs under, picking things up from the floor and explain clearly to them what they should do if you are still talking and the bell goes;

- develop rules for classroom talk – when is it allowed and when is it not?;

- develop clear rules for tasks – be clear about whether they should be working individually or whether they are allowed to collaborate;

- ensure that they do not eat food in lessons or chew gum;

- not permitting the wearing of hats or coats in the classroom;

- not permitting disrespect of school property – for example, by adding graffiti to their exercise books.

These are examples of classroom rules, but your school behaviour policy will guide you on the expectations. If you notice low-level disruption, 'nip this in the bud' immediately by challenging it. Ignoring it creates a culture of low expectations and often the problem will escalate if it is unchallenged.

PRAISE AND REWARDS

Take every opportunity to praise good behaviour and good effort in class, and by sending e-mails and text messages to parents. Assign rewards in line with the school policy. Although learners generally enjoy receiving praise and rewards, and their use results in other learners modifying their behaviour, there are some issues that you need to be aware of:

- the over-use of praise can result in a culture of low expectations, particularly when praise is given when it is not really deserved;

- it can result in learners working hard only because they want a reward; this promotes extrinsic motivation rather than intrinsic motivation;

- rewards and praise tend to be assigned to learners who do not demonstrate consistently good behaviour; when they suddenly modify their behaviour, they tend to receive praise or rewards;

- some learners never receive rewards or praise; these tend to be learners who work hard and behave well consistently.

CASE STUDY

A primary school leadership team worked with its staff to discuss and review the school's existing policies in relation to behaviour and engagement. The leadership team asked all staff to contribute to this process. They also invited the school's teacher training students to the consultation. The leaders were keen to gain an understanding of the perspectives of all staff, including those at different stages of their careers and with varied levels of experience.

Two experienced teachers, Emma and Hafid, had recently been appointed to their roles. During the review the leadership team asked Emma and Hafid to outline the policies that were used in their previous schools. Emma explained that the policy at her previous school placed greater emphasis on praise and recognition when compared to the policy at her current school. Hafid also shared a similar experience and stated that the policy at his previous school placed a much greater focus on rewards than it did on the use of sanctions.

The leadership team considered these comments and felt that the school was placing too much emphasis on the use of sanctions within the existing policy. They felt that this was at the expense of praise and recognition, and that a culture of reward had not been properly considered during previous policy consultations. All staff agreed that it was essential to have a clear policy on the use of sanctions, but that within the existing policy there was a clear need to further develop the focus on rewards.

In response to the consultation, the leadership team made a number of changes to the behaviour and engagement policy. These included:

- the introduction of a points system so that staff could reward positive behaviours;

- the introduction of an electronic communications tool so that learners' points totals could be accessed by parents through a secure website;

- the requirement of all staff to post a weekly praise certificate to one student of their choice;

- the introduction of a rewards and recognition assembly to celebrate successes and achievements;

- the use of 'weekly star' signs in classrooms and learning spaces.

Following the review and implementation of the policy, a number of parents contacted the school to provide feedback. Parents described the positive impact of the praise and recognition policy, and many stated how encouraging it had been for their child. Since its implementation, the school had seen a fall in the use of behaviour sanctions over a 12-month period and it continues to grow and embed this culture of recognition.

USING SANCTIONS

Sanctions should be applied either when learners' attitudes to learning are not good or when they demonstrate inappropriate behaviour. You must implement sanctions in line with school policy during your lessons, and sanctions should be proportionate to the incident that warranted their use.

CLASSROOM MANAGEMENT

One effective strategy for developing good classroom management is to implement a seating plan. This enables you to know learners' names quickly and to separate learners who are likely to disrupt each other. Follow the school policies on whether learners are allowed to leave their seats during lessons and school policy on toilet use during lessons. Make sure that your expectations are clear from the moment they enter the room. Giving them a task to do immediately is one way of settling them down and focusing them on learning.

PROMOTING POSITIVE LEARNING BEHAVIOUR

In recent years, there has been a move away from the term 'behaviour management' to 'behaviour for learning', despite the former term being adopted in the Teachers' Standards. Learners demonstrate good learning behaviour when they are:

- listening;
- collaborating;
- asking questions;
- challenging other people's opinions about subject content;
- persevering when they find something difficult;
- managing distractions;
- making connections between different aspects of learning;
- noticing;
- being independent;
- using tools for learning when they become 'stuck' rather than depending on a teacher.

Some learners find it difficult to participate in lessons. They do not ask questions and they tend to be passive. Quiet, passive and compliant behaviour is not good learning behaviour. You need to encourage your learners to ask questions, to affirm other people's responses or to challenge them, and to keep trying when they are working on a really difficult problem. Effective learners manage their distractions well. If there is disruption taking place, or if someone walks into the room to talk to you, effective learners manage these distractions well and continue with their task. Some learners waste valuable learning time when they become 'stuck' in their learning. This stops them from making progress in the lesson. Through teaching the learners a four-step process, you can offer them a framework to guide their response when this happens. When learners become 'stuck' you can encourage them to:

- **T**hink.

- **T**alk to a peer.

- Use **T**ools for learning (resources to help them with their learning).

- **T**alk to a teacher.

The four Ts approach ensures that the last thing they do if they become stuck is to ask a teacher. When you see learners demonstrating good learning behaviours you should provide positive descriptive praise – for example, 'I liked the way you persevered with that task, Sam'; 'I saw some really great collaboration in that group'.

KEY RESEARCH

Through operant conditioning, a child makes an association between a behaviour and a conse-quence (Skinner, 1938). The underlying principle is that positive reinforcement of good behaviour strengthens that behaviour. Positive reinforcement is best explained as the addition of a stimulus (reward) to increase the likelihood of a positive behaviour being repeated. Learners are rewarded for good behaviour and good work so that they will continue to demonstrate positive behaviour and produce high-quality work due to the likelihood of receiving the reward again. In classrooms, rewards may take the form of stickers, stamps, certificates or simply verbal praise. The problem with positive reinforcement is that it promotes extrinsic rather than intrinsic motivation. Learners demonstrate extrinsic motivation when they are only motivated to complete a task because of the reward that they will receive when the task has been completed. Intrinsic motivation is dem-onstrated when learners are motivated to complete a task because they enjoy the task, they are engaged by it and immersed in their learning. Most teachers want learners to be intrinsically motivated rather than extrinsically motivated. There is also a danger that 'empty' praise (praise when it is not really deserved) can foster a culture of low expectations (Coe et al., 2014).

In contrast, negative reinforcement (often incorrectly associated with punishment) is the removal of a negative stimulus to enable individuals to achieve their goals. The removal of a negative stimulus strengthens the likelihood of achieving the target goals. An example of negative rein-forcement is outlined as follows. A child with autistic spectrum conditions is completing a task in a mainstream classroom that provides sensory overload. The child finds it difficult to learn because the classroom is too noisy, and the child is distracted by the colourful displays. The child decides to go and work in a quiet study space. This is a space in the classroom which is sepa-rated by a partition so that the child can focus on their work without distraction. The child can complete the task successfully by removing the adverse stimulus (noise and colour).

(Continued)

(Continued)

Punishment can be positive or negative. Positive punishment is the addition of something that reduces the likelihood of the behaviour occurring again. Examples might include:

- the introduction of a report card system to monitor learners' behaviour in each lesson;

- a phone call home to parents to report poor behaviour.

Negative punishment is the removal of something to decrease the likelihood of behaviour occurring again. Examples include:

- the loss of break time;

- the loss of privileges;

- the loss of free time - e.g. detention;

- moving a child away from their friends in class.

The problem with behaviourist approaches is that they do not address the causes of behaviour. They only address consequences. Learners' behaviour is often rooted in social circumstances and their behaviour is often an attempt to communicate an unmet need. In contrast, humanist approaches assume that teachers need to pay attention to the needs of the whole child rather than simply focusing on consequences. Humanists such as Carl Rogers and Abraham Maslow are often viewed as the founding fathers of humanism. Rogers emphasised the need to build learners' self-esteem and the need for unconditional positive regard. Maslow, in his hierarchy of needs (Maslow, 1943), demonstrated how children cannot achieve their full potential unless their basic physiological needs, safety needs and their need to feel loved are addressed first.

CASE STUDY

The senior leaders of a secondary school in West Yorkshire led a staff voice activity to collect feedback from school staff in relation to their perceptions on behaviour and engagement. A range of teachers and leaders explained that they were concerned about persistent low-level negative behaviours and the impact of these on learners' engagement and progress. Some colleagues also explained that these behaviours were negatively impacting staff morale, mental health and well-being. In response to this feedback, the leaders planned and delivered a series of workshops to enable them to gain a deeper understanding of staff concerns. During these workshops, leaders also asked staff to contribute any ideas they had in relation to addressing and tackling low-level disruption.

The majority of teaching and classroom-based support staff felt that they had the necessary skills to address the majority of low-level negative behaviour.

These staff were asked to identify, compare and discuss the behaviour management approaches they currently used in their classrooms.

These approaches were written down and staff were then asked to group their ideas into common themes. The themes that they identified included:

- establishing and embedding routines linked to classroom entry and exit;

- the use of voice, presence and movement to avoid confrontation;

- the importance of sharing praise and recognition with both learners and parents;

- the modelling of good behaviours;

- asking targeted questions to refocus specific learners;

- using non-verbal communication;

- the role of lesson planning and its potential to impact on learners' engagement.

Teaching and classroom-based support staff agreed with leaders that it was important to maintain some freedom and autonomy in the use of these approaches. This ensured that behaviour management was contextual and responsive to the needs of classes and specific learners. However, they also agreed that some consistency across the school may support learners in recognising and responding to the expectations of staff regardless of the faculty or subject.

After a period of consultation and discussion, the school adapted and adopted a five Ps model. This model focuses on the importance of Praise, Pace, Purpose, Passion and Participation. Leaders explained that this model had been used successfully in other primary and secondary settings (DfE, 2017). It was agreed by all staff that this model would be used to structure and underpin the existing behaviour management practices of teachers and classroom-based support staff.

The model supports all teachers and classroom-based support staff with ensuring that a common approach underpins all lessons in order to further develop routine and consistency across the school. In summary, the model demonstrates five key elements of supporting behaviour and engagement through teaching and learning.

- Praise (the importance of all staff providing praise and recognition, and supporting learning through providing a positive classroom environment).

- Pace (recognising that good pace is essential to an effective lesson and the engagement of learners).

- Purpose (ensuring that every part of every lesson has a specific purpose and can be justified in relation to the sequencing and delivery of content).

- Passion (using energy, enthusiasm and passion to enthuse and engage learners).

- Participation (ensuring that there are frequent and meaningful opportunities for learners to engage with staff through discussion and questioning and, where appropriate, other learners).

After the implementation, leaders ensured that there were regular opportunities to review the implementation of the new policy and assess its impact on staff and learners. Additional refinements were often suggested and trialled either through pilot programmes or across the school. The five Ps model was used to support the school's culture of high expectation and teachers and classroom-based staff reported a reduction in low-level disruption.

PROFESSIONAL REFLECTION

Reflect on your own style for managing learners' behaviour. What are your preferred approaches and why do you like them? Reflect on approaches that you have observed that have been effective and less effective. What factors influenced the effectiveness of these approaches?

NEXT STEPS

Consider the extent to which your school policy promotes and fosters a culture of respect between learners, and between staff and learners. Reflect on your strengths and areas for development in relation to establishing and maintaining high expectations within your classroom. Discuss these with a colleague and exchange ideas. Think about the strategies and approaches that you use to promote positive learner behaviour and how you can further develop and embed the use of these. Seek advice and ideas from colleagues in school and follow social media channels to gain an awareness of the actions and ideas being trialled by professionals in other settings.

TAKE 5

- Think carefully about how your existing routines support learners' engagement and how you can further develop these.

- Identify the steps that you have taken to develop positive relationships with your learners. Consider how you could further develop these relationships.

- Focus on how you use reinforcement to influence behaviour.

- Try to identify your basic expectations of all learners. Think about how you share and enforce these and whether you can further develop your consistency.

- Reflect on the four Ts model and how you can use this to promote good learning behaviour.

WHAT HAVE YOU LEARNED?

This chapter has provided advice on how to manage learners' behaviour in lessons and how to promote good behaviour for learning. We have acknowledged that it is common for many teachers to feel anxious about learners' behaviour and that it is important to recognise that negative behaviour is usually not directed at you personally. In some cases, adverse childhood experiences may be affecting learners' behaviour and these individuals may have developed a poor sense of self as a result of these experiences. We have explained that it is important that teachers recognise that this can detrimentally impact on learner behaviour and that behavioural responses should not be taken personally. We have therefore emphasised that it is important that you try to understand the root causes of behaviour and that you ask for support whenever you feel that this would be valuable. However, we have also argued that it is important to recognise that teachers do have an influence on learners' behaviour and the chapter has outlined some important strategies that will support you with managing behaviour. The chapter has also discussed the importance of establishing high expectations and some practical guidance has been provided to support you in relation to developing relationships and positive attitudes to learning. It has also demonstrated the importance of establishing and embedding consistent rules and routines, and a few case studies have been provided to demonstrate some examples of effective practice in relation to classroom management. A range of critical questions have been asked to encourage you to reflect on your current practice, and identify strengths and areas for development.

FURTHER READING

Cowley, S (2014) *Getting the Buggers to Behave*. London: Bloomsbury.

Mortimer, H (2017) *Understanding Behaviour in Early Years Settings*. London: David Fulton Publishers.

6

THE FRAMEWORK: PERSONAL DEVELOPMENT

WHAT WILL YOU LEARN?

This chapter explores personal development within the context of the Education Inspection Framework (Ofsted, 2019) and it highlights the implications of this aspect of the framework for both school leadership teams and teachers. We argue that the curriculum plays a crucial role in relation to enriching learners' development and we provide some practical guidance to illuminate examples of effective practice. The chapter then emphasises the importance of a whole-school approach to character education and supporting learners to be mentally healthy. Additionally, we explore the mental health curriculum and provide some research and case study material to support you in reflecting on your existing provision. The chapter also provides some practical guidance to enable you to support learners to be physically healthy. Finally, it outlines guidance and suggests some practical strategies in relation to resilience, respect, diversity, citizenship and fundamental British values.

KEY POLICY

The Education Inspection Framework identifies 'personal development' as a separate strand that inspectors will evaluate. Inspectors will evaluate the extent to which:

- *the curriculum extends beyond the academic, technical or vocational. It provides for learners' broader development, enabling them to develop and discover their interests and talents;*

- *the curriculum and the school's wider work support learners to develop their character – including their resilience, confidence and independence – and help them know how to keep physically and mentally healthy;*

- *at each stage of education, the school prepares learners for future success in their next steps;*

- *the school prepares learners for life in modern Britain by: – equipping them to be responsible, respectful, active citizens who contribute positively to society – developing their understanding of fundamental British values – developing their understanding and appreciation of diversity – celebrating what we have in common and promoting respect for the different protected characteristics as defined in law.*

(Ofsted, 2019, p11)

A CURRICULUM THAT ENRICHES LEARNERS' DEVELOPMENT

The framework expects schools to provide learners with a broad curriculum in which they are given opportunities to study subjects in-depth. There is an expectation that the curriculum provides learners with opportunities to make connections between their learning in different subjects. In addition, primary schools should be providing children with access to the full breadth of the National Curriculum, and secondary schools that start learners on Key Stage 4 content too early (i.e. in Year 9 rather than Year 10) are likely to encounter criticism in inspections under the new framework. Secondary schools are expected to encourage more students to study the English Baccalaureate and to provide access to a broad, rich and deep curriculum in Key Stage 3.

In addition to the taught curriculum, schools will need to review their extra-curricular offer to ensure that it enables learners to develop a broad range of interests. Opportunities for learners to participate in residential activities, outdoor learning, voluntary work in the community and work experience will also contribute to learners' broader development. Schools should consider how they can provide students with opportunities to lead on initiatives. Examples include the development of a variety of roles, including peer mentors, mental health ambassadors, student ambassadors, student contributions to open days, student-led performances, conferences and opportunities for students to participate in debates about key issues. These activities contribute to learners' broader development by helping to shape their character.

DEVELOPING CHARACTER

Developing learners' characters is one of the key duties of schools. Positive character traits include:

- *the ability to remain motivated by long-term goals, to see a link between effort in the present and pay-off in the longer-term, overcoming and persevering through, and learning from, setbacks when encountered;*

- *the learning and habituation of positive moral attributes, sometimes known as 'virtues', and including, for example, courage, honesty, generosity, integrity, humility and a sense of justice, alongside others;*

- *sense of pride in the school and their work;*

- *good manners, courtesy, respect and good behaviour;*

- *the acquisition of social confidence and the ability to make points or arguments clearly and constructively, listen attentively to the views of others, behave with courtesy and good manners and speak persuasively to an audience;*

- *an appreciation of the importance of long-term commitments which frame the successful and fulfilled life, for example to spouse, partner, role or vocation, the local community, to faith or world view. This helps individuals to put down deep roots and gives stability and longevity to lifetime endeavours;*

- *high self-efficacy and self-belief;*

- *motivation;*

- *good self-control (or self-regulation, the ability to delay gratification);*

- *coping skills (part of being able to bounce back).*

(DfE, 2019a)

Schools that develop character will help drive equity and promote social mobility for their learners. A carefully designed curriculum ensures that learners grow in self-confidence in their ability to learn and make progress in mastering appropriately challenging subject content.

Schools can develop character through providing a rich curriculum and extra-curricular offer, which includes opportunities for volunteering, performing and debating. Opportunities for learners to work in and with the community can promote civic pride within students.

SUPPORTING LEARNERS TO BE MENTALLY HEALTHY

Evidence suggests that there is a growing mental health crisis in children and young people. Approximately one in ten children and young people has a diagnosable mental health need (DfE/DoH, 2017) and some young people are more vulnerable than others. The causes of mental ill health in young people are complex and multifaceted. Risk factors are rooted within individuals, families, communities and poverty (Glazzard, 2019). In England, waiting lists to access specialist external support are long and the threshold criteria to secure a referral for a child to gain clinical support are stringent, resulting in many young people not meeting the criteria for a referral.

Within this context, schools have been positioned as playing a fundamental role in supporting young people's mental health. Mental health exists along a continuum, which ranges from being mentally healthy to being mentally ill. The definition by the World Health Organization (WHO) defines mental health as *a state of well-being in which the individual realizes his or her own abilities, can cope with the normal stresses of life, can work productively and fruitfully, and is able to make a contribution to his or her community* (WHO, 2004). So, what is the role of schools in supporting children and young people to stay mentally healthy?

The whole-school approach to mental health outlined by Public Health England (2015) outlines the key components of the whole-school approach. These are outlined below:

- *Leadership and management: the senior leadership team must prioritise the well-being of learners and staff. Mental health should be a key strategic priority and a focus for leadership meetings, governors' meetings, the school self-evaluation and school improvement plan.*

- *There should be a positive culture in schools and classrooms which promotes a sense of belonging and mutual respect between children and adults, between adults and between children.*

- *Learners should be provided with a mental health curriculum which enables them to develop emotional and social regulation skills, resilience and their knowledge of mental health.*

- *Staff working in schools need access to high-quality professional development which enables them to identify the signs and symptoms of mental ill health.*

- *There should be a clear approach for the identification of mental health needs in children and young people. This approach should be proactive so that young people who do not display visible signs of mental ill health are identified.*

- *Schools should be aware that parents of children with mental ill health may also have mental health problems. A key component of the whole-school approach to mental health should ensure that parents are given the support they need to support their own mental health and the mental health of their children.*

- *Schools should provide a planned programme of interventions for small groups of learners and individuals with specific mental health needs.*

- *Schools should develop a clear policy for referring children to external services which clearly outlines the steps to be taken.*

(DoH, 2015)

DEVELOPING A MENTAL HEALTH CURRICULUM

One of the expectations of the Education Inspection Framework is that schools will provide learners with a mental health curriculum that develops their mental health literacy. A well-planned mental health curriculum should aim to develop young people's social and emotional regulation skills (Roffey, 2017), their resilience, their knowledge of mental health conditions and it should provide them with strategies for managing their own mental health.

The mental health curriculum should be sequenced appropriately across the early years, primary and secondary phases so that learners develop cumulative and age-appropriate knowledge. Typically, in the early years an effective mental health curriculum is designed to educate children about different types of emotions so that they develop emotional literacy. Children need to be able to recognise the emotions they are experiencing, but also how to regulate these. Therefore, they need to learn strategies that they can implement when they are feeling lonely, sad or angry. The ability to control our emotions within specific contexts is a critical skill for young people to develop. In addition, young children also need to learn about social skills and how these might be affected by the different contexts that they move between. They need to understand, for example, that social behaviours that may be acceptable in an informal context might not be acceptable within school or other professional contexts. As learners progress through primary school and into secondary school, they need to learn about different mental health conditions, including stress, anxiety, depression, self-harm, gaming and eating disorders. They need to understand how to manage these conditions if they experience them, and thus, a mental health curriculum should aim to provide young people with a range of strategies that can be adopted if they experience mental ill health. Examples include mindfulness, exercises for regulating one's breathing, engagement in physical activity and developing social connections.

Teachers should encourage young people to talk about how they feel, thus destigmatising mental health. Boys may be reluctant to express their feelings or emotions, and teachers should work hard to encourage them to do this. Learning about how to access support should be a key component of the mental health curriculum, and schools should ensure that young people are aware of the support that they can access both in the school and in the community.

The mental health curriculum should address the link between social media and mental health. This relationship is now well established in the academic literature (Frith, 2017) and young people need to be taught about the risks that they might encounter online and ways of mitigating these. Additionally, learners need to understand their responsibilities as digital citizens (Glazzard and Stones, 2019) within the online world. They need to be taught how to stay within the limits of the law and they need to learn about how to be digitally resilient.

Evidence from research (Glazzard, 2019) suggests that primary school teachers prefer to avoid using the term 'mental health' with young children. This could be because they feel that the term 'mental health' is potentially somehow damaging to young children. Instead, they prefer to use softer terms such as 'feelings' and 'emotions'. The problem with this is that these attitudes help to perpetuate the stigma associated with mental health. If young children are able to learn about looking after their physical health, they also need to learn about looking after their mental health. They need to learn the importance of looking after their body *and* their mind.

The inclusion of mental health in the Education Inspection Framework is a positive development. However, it is disappointing that it does not form a component of the judgement on leadership and management. This is because schools need to address mental health strategically through the implementation of a whole-school approach. If this is embedded, then it should reduce the likelihood of children developing serious mental health problems.

Although schools are well placed to support children and young people's mental health, it is important to remember that the root causes of mental ill health lie in social circumstances. Therefore, to reverse the mental health crisis, the government also needs to provide a systemic response that addresses the systemic factors that cause mental ill-health in the first place. These factors include poverty, adverse childhood experiences, the National Curriculum and the assessment systems to which young people are subjected. These broader factors lie outside the control of schools, yet schools are positioned as a potential solution to the mental health crisis. Schools cannot and should not be expected to solve societal problems and teachers are not mental health experts. Therefore, there is a limit to the type of interventions that school can provide. Greater collaboration between education, health and social services is necessary to address this complex aspect of the inspection framework.

CASE STUDY

A primary school developed the role of mental health champions. Students had to apply for the role and they were interviewed for it. Those who were selected were chosen for their maturity and other positive character traits such as empathy, patience and integrity. The mental health champions completed a training course in sensitive listening. They were taught how to be good listeners, the skills associated with effective listening, the importance of confidentiality and when to refer cases to adults. They were subsequently matched to specific children who needed a friendly 'listening ear'.

SUPPORTING LEARNERS TO BE PHYSICALLY HEALTHY

Physical activity is essential for a healthy life and there is an established association between physical activity and mental health (Glazzard et al., 2019). Thus, physical activity improves mental health as well as reducing obesity and increasing mental alertness.

Schools should ensure that all learners are able to benefit from physical activity. One way of addressing this is for schools to provide learners with a broad physical education curriculum so that young people can enjoy participating in something they enjoy. Some children might not enjoy team sports, but may enjoy individual sports. Children with autistic spectrum conditions might experience heightened states of anxiety if they are required to participate in a team sport. These learners might not enjoy competitive sports or sports that cause them to get hot and sweaty. This is due to their sensory sensitivities. Individual sports, including climbing, boxing, swimming and moving on a treadmill, might be preferable to some learners than team sports. Many primary schools now engage children in the 'daily mile'. The children complete one mile of physical activity each day during school time. This can be broken up into shorter periods of physical activity or completed in a single time-frame.

The physical education curriculum should aim to foster a love of physical activity so that learners engage in physical activity outside of school and also view physical activity as an essential component of a healthy lifestyle. Schools should therefore consider ways of including learners who identify as lesbian, gay, bisexual or transgender in physical education so that they experience a sense of belonging rather than being exposed to a heteronormative environment.

DEVELOPING RESILIENCE

Resilience is often conceptualised as 'bouncing back' from situations of adversity. However, the concept of 'bounce-back' is problematic because some learners might have experienced significant trauma that may have left deep emotional scars (Roffey, 2017). It is not always easy to bounce back from traumatic situations. In addition, although resilience is often seen as being an individual characteristic, it is relational (Roffey, 2017). Children and young people are more likely to demonstrate greater resilience if they have support from peers, family members and teachers. Access to supportive social networks can increase resilience. In addition, resilience is influenced by the contexts that we inhabit (Roffey, 2017). It is possible for children to be resilient in some contexts but not resilient in others. Some children may be resilient if they are playing in a team game, but they may also demonstrate a lack of resilience when they are attempting to solve a mathematical problem. They may be resilient in social networks but demonstrate a lack of resilience in their academic learning.

You will need to consider how you can promote children's resilience within the context of your classroom. It is important that you emphasise to your students that learning is hard. In fact, when people are operating at the very limits of their capability, learning is extremely hard. It is important that learners understand that everyone experiences this when they are learning. It is important that they know that you also find some learning hard. It is important that they know that, with perseverance and effort, they will eventually be able to master the thing they are finding difficult. You should therefore encourage your learners to persevere with challenging tasks.

Learners also need to be resilient to the feedback that you provide. They need to understand that the feedback is designed to be constructive and to support their development. Although you should aim to provide constructive feedback on students' work, it is also important that you identify ways in which they can improve it. Resilient learners understand that feedback serves this purpose and they can use feedback to progress further in their development.

PREPARING LEARNERS FOR THE NEXT STAGE

A well-planned curriculum should ensure that learners are prepared for the next stage of their journey, whether this is within education, employment or training. There should be a seamless transition to the next stage in learners' development. Thus, transitions to the next stage should be supported by a range of strategies, including taster days and transition days. Abrupt transitions can result in young people developing mental ill-health and this can have a detrimental effect on their learning and development. In addition, the taught curriculum should prepare learners adequately for their next stage in education, employment and training.

DEVELOPING CITIZENSHIP

Citizenship and character education are closely interrelated. Essentially, the curriculum should be designed so that learners understand the concept of citizenship. They need to understand what it means to be a good citizen both in the offline and online worlds. Although the concept of digital citizenship is relatively new, it is vital that learners understand that there should be no difference in how they conduct themselves in both the offline and online worlds. Given the prevalence of cyberbullying, the need for young people to understand the concept of digital citizenship cannot be over-emphasised. Learners need to understand the importance of treating others with respect and demonstrating empathy, and they need to understand the potential harmful effects of their words and actions. The guidance from the Department for Education is stated below.

During key stage 1 pupils learn about themselves as developing individuals and as members of their communities, building on their own experiences and on the early learning goals for personal, social and emotional development. They learn the basic rules and skills for keeping themselves healthy and safe and for behaving well. They have opportunities to show they can take some responsibility for themselves and their environment. They begin to learn about their own and other people's feelings and become aware of the views, needs and rights of other children and older people. As members of a class and school community, they learn social skills such as how to share, take turns, play, help others, resolve simple arguments and resist bullying. They begin to take an active part in the life of their school and its neighbourhood.

During key stage 2 pupils learn about themselves as growing and changing individuals with their own experiences and ideas, and as members of their communities. They become more mature, independent and self-confident. They learn about the wider world and the interdependence of communities within it. They develop their sense of social justice and moral responsibility and begin to understand that their own choices and behaviour can affect local, national or global issues and political and social institutions. They learn how to take part more fully in school and community activities. As they begin to develop into young adults, they face the changes of puberty and transfer to secondary school with support and encouragement from their school. They learn how to make more confident and informed choices about their health and environment; to take more responsibility, individually and as a group, for their own learning; and to resist bullying.

(DfE, 2015)

In secondary schools the guidance states that in Key Stage 3:

Teaching should develop pupils' understanding of democracy, government and the rights and responsibilities of citizens. Pupils should use and apply their knowledge and understanding whilst developing skills to research and interrogate evidence, debate and evaluate viewpoints, present reasoned arguments and take informed action. Pupils should be taught about:

- *the development of the political system of democratic government in the United Kingdom, including the roles of citizens, Parliament and the monarch;*

- *the operation of Parliament, including voting and elections, and the role of political parties;*

- *the precious liberties enjoyed by the citizens of the United Kingdom;*

- *the nature of rules and laws and the justice system, including the role of the police and the operation of courts and tribunals;*

- *the roles played by public institutions and voluntary groups in society, and the ways in which citizens work together to improve their communities, including opportunities to participate in school-based activities;*

- *the functions and uses of money, the importance and practice of budgeting, and managing risk.*

(DfE, 2013)

At Key Stage 4:

Teaching should build on the key stage 3 programme of study to deepen pupils' understanding of democracy, government and the rights and responsibilities of citizens. Pupils should develop their skills to be able to use a range of research strategies, weigh up evidence, make persuasive arguments and substantiate their conclusions. They should experience and evaluate different ways that citizens can act together to solve problems and contribute to society.

Pupils should be taught about:

- *parliamentary democracy and the key elements of the constitution of the United Kingdom, including the power of government, the role of citizens and Parliament in holding those in power to account, and the different roles of the executive, legislature and judiciary and a free press;*

- *the different electoral systems used in and beyond the United Kingdom and actions citizens can take in democratic and electoral processes to influence decisions locally, nationally and beyond;*

- *other systems and forms of government, both democratic and non-democratic, beyond the United Kingdom.*

(DfE, 2013)

DEVELOPING AN UNDERSTANDING OF DIVERSITY AND PROMOTING RESPECT

The curriculum should be carefully designed to address Section 149 of the Equality Act (2010) which requires schools to foster good relations between different groups and protect those with protected characteristics from discrimination. You should therefore seek opportunities to integrate issues pertaining to race, religion, sexuality, gender identity and disability into the subjects that you teach. You should be prepared to challenge all forms of harassment, discrimination and prejudice, including micro-aggressions. These are usually non-verbal subtle forms of prejudice and discrimination that can occur in classrooms. Your classroom environment should reflect the diversity of your learners, and the resources that you use to support your teaching should also reflect diversity.

PROMOTING FUNDAMENTAL BRITISH VALUES

The fundamental British values include democracy, the rule of law, individual liberty and mutual respect, and tolerance of those with different faiths and beliefs (DfE, 2011). They are an integral part of the teachers' standards and a component of the Education Inspection Framework (Ofsted, 2019).

So, how can you promote these in your teaching? Activities such as voting support children's understanding of democracy. This can be further enhanced by participating in debates and visits to the Houses of Parliament. You should promote mutual respect in all lessons and challenge learners when respect is not demonstrated. A well-planned and sequenced religious education curriculum will ensure that learners develop a solid understanding of different religious beliefs and it will promote respect and tolerance of different faiths and beliefs. Opportunities for learners to develop religious and cultural awareness should be embedded across the curriculum.

CASE STUDY

Secondary schools in one local authority worked with the local football club to design a mental health curriculum programme that would be delivered to all students in Year 8 by sports coaches employed by the club. The coaches were trained by an outside company to support them in the development of their subject and pedagogical knowledge. The curriculum included an introductory session on mental health. It then progressed to include lessons on stress, anxiety, depression, resilience, social media and how to be a good listener. The programme was evaluated by a local university. A mental health literacy survey was used to evaluate the students' knowledge of mental health before and after the intervention. Focus group interviews were also conducted with the students. The evaluation revealed that the students' mental health literacy scores increased. The interviews demonstrated that the students were able to identify strategies for managing their own mental health and able to identify how they would seek help should they need it.

KEY RESEARCH

Research suggests that relationships between staff and students, and between students, are critical in promoting student well-being and in helping to engender a sense of belonging to the school (Calear and Christensen, 2010).

The personal, social and emotional (PSE) curriculum in the school can impact positively on young people's health and well-being, as well as providing them with the skills they need (Durlak et al., 2014; Goodman et al., 2015). An essential element of a whole-school approach to mental health is the development of a curriculum that provides children and young people with knowledge of mental health in order to improve their own mental health literacy.

The term 'mental health literacy' was first introduced by Jorm and colleagues and is defined as *knowledge and beliefs about mental disorders which aid their recognition, management and prevention* (Jorm et al., 1997, p184). It is known that young people in particular have low levels of mental health literacy – i.e. they have difficulties in identifying mental disorders and their underlying causes, risk factors and associated protective factors, and can develop incorrect beliefs about the effectiveness of therapeutic interventions (Jorm et al., 2006; Kelly et al., 2007). Additionally, the stigma associated with mental health problems becomes apparent to people at an early age (Campos et al., 2018). However, research suggests that the attitudes of young people can be changed more easily than those of adults (Corrigan and Watson, 2007) and therefore schools can play a critical role in improving young people's mental health literacy through the introduction of curriculum programmes that are specifically designed to develop young people's knowledge about mental health and shape the development of positive attitudes towards it, thus reducing stigma. Research has demonstrated that young women have higher levels of mental health literacy than boys (Martínez-Zambrano et al., 2013). This could be because girls may be more willing to engage in help-seeking behaviours such as receiving advice in relation to their mental health.

PROFESSIONAL REFLECTION

Reflect on the subject(s) that you teach. What are the opportunities for developing learners' understanding of citizenship, mental health and inclusion in the units that you teach?

NEXT STEPS

Now plan opportunities to develop learners' personal development through the subject(s) that you teach. Talk to colleagues who work in the pastoral team to find out more about their roles and responsibilities.

TAKE 5

- Learners need to be taught a mental health curriculum that promotes the skills of emotional and social regulation.
- Learners need an education that supports them with the development of character, but character education also needs to be embedded throughout the curriculum.
- Physical activity supports young people to be mentally healthy.
- The curriculum should promote fundamental British values across all subjects.
- The curriculum should be designed to support the development of resilience within learners.

WHAT HAVE YOU LEARNED?

In this chapter we have emphasised the importance of providing a curriculum that enables young people to be physically and mentally healthy. We have emphasised that the development of resilience is a key skill, but we have also argued that resilience is context-specific and relational. We have outlined the importance of designing a curriculum that supports the development of positive character traits, and we have stressed the role that the curriculum plays in developing inclusive attitudes and values in young people.

FURTHER READING

Glazzard, J Potter, M and Stones, S (2019) *Meeting the Mental Health Needs of Young Children 0–5 years*. St Albans: Critical Publishing.

Glazzard, J and Bancroft, K (2018) *Meeting the Mental Health Needs of Learners 11–18 Years (Positive Mental Health)*. St Albans: Critical Publishing.

Glazzard, J and Trussler, S (2018) *Supporting Mental Health in Primary and Early Years: A Practice-based Approach*. London: Sage.

7

THE FRAMEWORK: LEADERSHIP AND MANAGEMENT

WHAT WILL YOU LEARN?

This chapter demonstrates effective practices of leadership and management within the context of the Education Inspection Framework (Ofsted, 2019). In doing so, it addresses the requirements of the inspection process in relation to this aspect of the new framework. The chapter emphasises the importance of senior leaders committing to the provision of an ambitious curriculum and we provide some discussion to exemplify effective practice. Additionally, the chapter outlines leaders' responsibilities in relation to the professional development of staff. Some guidance is provided to support leaders to understand the concepts of 'gaming' and 'off-rolling'. Within this guidance we emphasise the importance of leaders working to ensure that all learners complete their programmes of study. The chapter then outlines leaders' responsibilities in relation to working with the community, reducing unnecessary workload and developing a positive culture. The role of school governors is discussed and through this discussion we highlight the roles and responsibilities of the governing body in relation to accountability. Practical guidance is then offered to support leaders to develop a culture of safeguarding through reflecting on existing provision within the school context.

KEY POLICY

According to the Education Inspection Framework, inspectors will evaluate the extent to which:

- *leaders have a clear and ambitious vision for providing high-quality, inclusive education and training to all. This is realised through strong, shared values, policies and practice;*

- *leaders focus on improving staff's subject, pedagogical and pedagogical content knowledge to enhance the teaching of the curriculum and the appropriate use of assessment;*

- *leaders aim to ensure that all learners complete their programmes of study. They provide the support for staff to make this possible and do not allow gaming or off-rolling;*

- *leaders engage effectively with learners and others in their community, including – where relevant – parents, carers, employers and local services;*

- *leaders engage with their staff and are aware and take account of the main pressures on them. They are realistic and constructive in the way that they manage staff, including their workload;*

- *leaders protect their staff from bullying and harassment;*

- *those responsible for governance understand their role and carry this out effectively. They ensure that the provider has a clear vision and strategy and that resources are managed well. They hold leaders to account for the quality of education or training;*

- *those with responsibility for governance ensure that the provider fulfils its statutory duties, for example under the Equality Act 2010, and other duties, for example in relation to the 'Prevent' strategy and safeguarding, and promoting the welfare of learners;*

- *the provider has a culture of safeguarding that supports effective arrangements to:*

  o *identify learners who may need early help or who are at risk of neglect, abuse, grooming or exploitation;*

  o *help learners reduce their risk of harm by securing the support they need, or referring in a timely way to those who have the expertise to help;*

  o *manage safe recruitment and allegations about adults who may be a risk to learners and vulnerable adults;*

- *Inspectors will always report on whether arrangements for safeguarding learners are effective.*

DEVELOPING AN AMBITIOUS VISION

Senior leaders need to demonstrate that their vision for the school is underpinned by high expectations of all learners regardless of social background, special educational needs and other circumstances which can detrimentally impact on academic attainment. Leaders need to be able to demonstrate that the vision for the school is inclusive and that it secures learners' entitlement to a high-quality education. The vision statement should be underpinned by a set of values to which all stakeholders have contributed. Leaders should ensure that policies are consistently implemented, and it is therefore your responsibility as a teacher to adhere to school policies, regardless of whether you agree with them.

PROVIDING PROFESSIONAL DEVELOPMENT

One of the key responsibilities of school leaders is to develop teachers to enable them to be the very best they can be. School leaders should take responsibility for sourcing professional development opportunities. As a teacher, you may also identify professional development courses that you wish to undertake, either because it will support you in addressing identified needs or because it will provide you with opportunities to advance your career. In the context of increasingly restricted school budgets, school leaders may need to prioritise professional development courses that help teachers to address the priorities on the school improvement plan. However, where possible, leaders should support teachers who have identified professional development opportunities because this is one way of retaining high-quality teachers in school. Many schools are increasingly supporting teachers who wish to study for higher degrees for career advancement reasons.

One-off professional development courses are unlikely to be as effective as courses that require teachers to attend a series of sessions with gaps in between sessions to allow teachers to put the ideas from the training into practice. In professional development sessions, teachers can then share their practice with colleagues and engage in a continuous cycle of reflection.

Some leaders develop a plan of professional development sessions at the beginning of the academic year. Others develop a more flexible approach to planning professional development which is responsive to the outcomes of the monitoring processes that take place during the year. Themes arising from the monitoring of lesson observations, conversations and feedback from learners and work sampling can be used to identify whole-school professional development priorities at specific stages during the academic year. Themes from whole-school monitoring can be used to inform a generic professional development programme, and specific themes arising from the monitoring of an individual teacher should be used to identify bespoke and targeted professional development for that individual.

The purpose of professional development should be to develop teachers and improve teaching in classrooms. This should have a positive impact on outcomes for learners. Senior leaders therefore need to monitor systematically the impact of teacher professional development on the quality of teaching and student outcomes to determine whether the investment made was good value for money.

In-house professional development that specifically addresses the needs of the school is likely to be more effective than externally sourced professional development.

Each school has a wealth of professional talent and it is valuable for staff working in the school to lead professional development for other staff. Coaching is a particularly effective form of professional development, which many schools now use to support teacher development.

GAMING AND OFF-ROLLING

During the inspection process, inspectors will challenge leaders and managers in relation to any unusual patterns of data or examination entry that have appeared to *game the system* (Ofsted, 2019). This will include entering learners for qualifications that are not in their educational best interests (but are likely to be in the school's best interests) and entering learners for similar qualifications that offer a significant overlap in terms of subject content. Inspectors will use historical data to determine whether it is likely that gaming has taken place. If inspectors uncover evidence of deliberate or substantial gaming, then any subsequent judgement in relation to leadership and management will be inadequate.

This rigorous approach is important in order to ensure that schools are offering a curriculum that meets and reflects their learners' needs. Schools that attempt to game the system are making decisions about the curriculum provision which are designed to favour league tables and outcomes rather than the needs of the learners in that setting. All learners are entitled to a broad and balanced curriculum which is ambitious in its aims. A school that attempts to game the system through this narrowing of the curriculum offer cannot fulfil its responsibility to the learners in its care.

The Education Inspection Framework also considers 'off-rolling' as a form of gaming. In the new framework, Ofsted provides a useful explanation of practices that constitute off-rolling in these circumstances:

> *The practice of removing a learner from the provider's roll without a formal, permanent exclusion or by encouraging a parent to remove their child, when the removal is primarily in the interests of the provider rather than in the best interests of the learner.*

> (Ofsted, 2019)

There is no circumstance in which Ofsted will believe that the use of off-rolling is acceptable or justified. However, it is important to recognise common situations and scenarios that are acceptable and justified, and therefore do not constitute off-rolling. In summary, these include learners who have left their school or moved to a new school because:

- the learner has left the country;
- the learner has moved to a new house;

- there is a school that is closer to the learner's home and it has a place available;

- the learner is being home-educated (and this is a parental choice made without the pressure or influence of the school);

- the learner has been dual registered with another school – for example, an alternative provider.

In some cases, the school may move a learner from one setting to another setting as an attempt to stop or interrupt an established cycle of poor behaviour. Leaders have a responsibility to ensure that this 'managed move' is in the best interests of the learner and that it is not being made to benefit the school or its outcomes. Leaders must also ensure that these moves only happen with the agreement of all of those involved, and they must follow statutory guidance in order to ensure that this process is not regarded as off-rolling.

It is also worth considering permanent exclusion as a reason for a learner leaving a school. Ofsted supports the use of permanent exclusion as long as headteachers have followed all legislation and statutory guidance. The permanent exclusion must also be a part of the school's behaviour policy and used as a last resort. In these cases, the use of permanent exclusion is acceptable and will not be considered by Ofsted as a form of gaming or off-rolling.

Ofsted analyses data on pupil movements to support the decisions that they make in relation to the inspection of schools. During the inspection process, inspectors will ask leaders to explain any exceptional levels of pupil movement in the school. Ofsted also analyses the movement of learners with special educational needs and disabilities, and will communicate with local authorities and multi-academy trusts about pupil movement in their area and in their schools.

Disadvantaged learners, learners with special educational needs and learners with low prior attainment are disproportionately off-rolled by schools. During the inspection process, inspectors will ask leaders to provide details confirming who has left the school and why this has been the case. If inspectors identify patterns, then they may examine the school's provision in relation to the support that is offered to learners in these groups. A school that is found to be involved in the off-rolling of a learner or its learners is likely to be judged as inadequate for leadership and management. Off-rolling does not put a learner's welfare or their quality of education first, and it is therefore right that Ofsted are taking serious action to address this practice.

WORKING WITH THE COMMUNITY

Schools are a fundamental part of the communities that they serve. Senior leaders need to consider ways of strengthening relationships with parents and other members of the community. The following suggestions provide useful starting points for working with the community.

- Involve parents in the primary classroom to support learning – for example, supporting reading development.

- Provide workshops for parents on specific teaching approaches to enable them to support their child's learning at home.

- Provide parental workshops on mental health and well-being to support parents in managing their own mental health and the mental health of their child.

- Consult with parents on key policies, including Relationships and Sex Education and behaviour management.

- Seek regular feedback from parents to elicit their views on the quality of education and act on their feedback where possible.

- Provide literacy classes for parents, particularly those who do not speak English.

- Provide opportunities for young people to undertake voluntary work and fundraising in the community.

- Invite key people from the community to come into school to deliver presentations and lessons – for example, religious leaders, local authors, poets and artists, and those from local businesses.

- Plan opportunities for young people to take action to address community issues – for example, participating in picking up litter.

- Provide work experience for learners in local businesses.

- Involve fathers in school life by asking them to come into school to support children's learning. This helps to break down gender stereotypes.

- Provide workshops for parents to support them into employment – for example, by leading sessions on writing job applications, providing voluntary work in schools for parents to support their curriculum vitae and provide workshops on budgeting and managing finances.

- Provide workshops for parents to support them in understanding the range of technological applications that their children are using.

- Develop strong partnerships with local businesses and universities. Arrange visits to these so that learners can experience a range of context.

- Develop clear methods of communication with parents, including making effective use of the school's virtual platform to communicate information.

- Invite the community into school for celebration events.

REDUCING UNNECESSARY WORKLOAD

Workload demands are one of the key factors that result in stress for teachers and excessive workload results in teacher attrition. Senior leaders must now take steps to reduce unnecessary planning, assessment and data management so that teachers can focus on teaching rather than fulfilling bureaucratic demands. The Department for Education has been focusing on this issue for the last two years and the Education Inspection Framework now includes the issue of workload within the judgement on leadership and management. Inspectors will evaluate the extent to which leaders are taking steps to reduce workload. Workload demands should be reasonable and proportionate to the roles that staff are undertaking. It is important that teachers are not being required to complete paperwork just for the purposes of Ofsted inspections, because inspectors do not expect paperwork to be generated solely to satisfy inspectors.

Leaders should therefore have a clear rationale for workload tasks that teachers are asked to complete. Inspectors do not expect to see planning in any particular format and inspectors do not expect marking to follow a specific model. We have addressed the myths about planning, assessment and data management in Chapter 2. Leaders should reasonably expect teachers to complete tasks that have a direct impact on the progress of learners. If workload tasks do not impact directly on learners – for example, if the task is only being done to satisfy leaders – then teachers have a right to question this. Placing staff under additional and unnecessary pressures is not acceptable and takes their time away from focusing on teaching and learning.

Other ways of reducing workload and stress include the following:

- *Limit communications to staff: collate messages into one communication rather than sending out multiple e-mails.*

- *Set restrictions on use of e-mail outside the working day.*

- *Reduce the number of meetings that staff need to attend or shorten meetings if they are necessary.*

- *Review the way that students' reports are written to check that they do not place unreasonable demands on teachers.*

(DfE, 2019a)

KEY RESEARCH

Research by the Education Support Partnership demonstrates the following:

- *72% of all educational professionals described themselves as stressed (84% of senior leaders).*

- *57% More than half of all education professionals have considered leaving the sector over the past two years due to pressures on their health and wellbeing.*

- *78% of all education professionals have experienced behavioural, psychological or physical symptoms due to their work.*

- *71% of education professionals cited workload as the main reason for considering leaving their jobs.*

(ESP, 2019)

DEVELOPING A POSITIVE CULTURE

Leaders should create a positive school culture in which staff and learners can thrive. Schools should be environments in which members of that community are valued, trusted and treated with respect. Individuals should experience a sense of belonging and enjoy going in every day. In evaluating your school culture consider the following.

- How do staff communicate with other members of staff?

- Does the leadership team demonstrate compassionate, ethical and authentic leadership?

- How do staff communicate with learners?

- How do learners communicate with staff?

- How do young people communicate with each other?

- Is there any bullying? If so, how is this being addressed?

- Does the physical environment (e.g. displays) reflect the diversity of the student and staff population? What messages do the notices and images on the walls say about the school culture?

- Do the resources reflect different forms of diversity?

- Are the views of learners, parents and staff sought and, if so, are they acted upon?

TEACHING WELLBEING

Research by the Education Support Partnership demonstrates the following:

72%

of all educational professionals described themselves as stressed (84% of senior leaders).

57%

More than half of all education professionals have considered leaving the sector over the past two years due to pressures on their health and wellbeing.

78%

of all education professionals have experienced behavioural, psychological or physical symptoms due to their work.

71%

of education professionals cited workload as the main reason for considering leaving their jobs.

Reference:
Education Support Partnership, (ESP), (2019), Teacher Wellbeing Index, 2019, London: ESP.

- How well does the school work in partnership with the community?

- Are students and parents treated as partners and what mechanisms are in place to demonstrate these partnerships?

- To what extent does the curriculum reflect the identities and interests of the learners?

- Is there a whole-school strategy for mental health and well-being?

- Is there a whole-school strategy for staff well-being?

- Is there a caring ethos?

- Is the physical environment looked after, clean and tidy?

- Are the vision and values statements visible and do they reflect a commitment to inclusion?

- Is there a calm atmosphere so that the school feels like a safe place?

THE ROLE OF SCHOOL GOVERNORS

Governors form part of the leadership and management of the schools. The role of the Governing Body is to ratify the school policies, monitor the effectiveness of the school and provide appropriate challenge to the school leaders. The role of the Governing Body is to essentially hold the school leaders to account. They play an important role in monitoring the quality of teaching and academic standards, and also in monitoring that the school funds are being appropriately and sensibly spent.

Inspectors will be interested in the level of challenge that governors present during meetings. They will ask to review the minutes of governors' meetings to check that governors are holding the leaders to account by providing an appropriate level of challenge. The Governing Body is a strategic body that serves a monitoring purpose. Although governors should not get involved in day-to-day operational matters, they do need to know what is happening in the school. They are not in post to represent their individual interests, but they are there to serve the interests of the whole school.

SAFEGUARDING

Inspectors will evaluate the extent to which the school meets its statutory safeguarding responsibilities. These are clearly outlined in *Keeping Children Safe in Education: Statutory Guidance for Schools and Colleges* (DfE, 2019b). Inspectors will also evaluate the extent to which the school keeps children and young people safe by preventing bullying. Inspectors will review school behaviour records of logged incidents to check that incidents have been properly addressed and closed down. They will check specifically for racist bullying and homophobic, biphobic and transphobic bullying. Inspectors will evaluate the extent to which schools meet their legal duties in relation to the Equality Act (2010) to protect learners with specific protected characteristics from direct and indirect discrimination. They will be interested in exploring how the school educates young people about knife crime and other forms of violent crime. Inspectors will also interrogate school exclusion records to ensure that decisions have been made fairly. They will explore the curriculum offer in relation to Prevent and e-safety.

CASE STUDY

The senior leadership teams of two nearby primary schools introduced a collaborative project to provide opportunities for teachers to work together. The senior leaders agreed to introduce this project following an audit of each school's strengths and areas for development. This audit identified the need for senior leaders to place a greater emphasis on the professional development of teachers.

The senior leadership teams provided dedicated development time for teachers to work together and identify training needs in relation to subject knowledge. Each teacher was asked to identify their own strengths and areas for development, and these were used to create training and development groups in which teachers could exchange and discuss subject knowledge. These sessions were also supported by subject associations and subject experts from the local secondary school. The programme supported teachers to strengthen their existing subject knowledge while providing tailored and individualised professional development opportunities. The project also strengthened relationships between schools and with the subject associations involved.

CASE STUDY

A secondary school leadership team asked teachers to provide feedback in relation to their perspectives on assessment and data management. The teachers were also asked to explain the impact of these activities on their well-being and workload. The feedback that the leaders collected demonstrated concerns in relation to managing assessment and being able to balance these demands with other aspects of their roles. Several staff felt that the time spent marking work was not effective and that time could be better spent on planning activities. The leadership team reviewed the school assessment policy and created an opportunity for staff to contribute to this review. Within the new policy it was agreed that teaching staff should provide pupils with high-quality verbal feedback during lessons and only provide written feedback when there was a sound educational reason to do so. The policy also stated that teachers should identify when it is appropriate to use book sampling (looking at a sample of books, rather than a complete set) as an alternative to providing written feedback to all learners. The policy explained that this allows teachers to provide feedback to learners by highlighting learners' misconceptions while reducing teacher workload. Leaders and teachers agreed that written feedback was still an essential part of the assessment cycle and that it was important for teachers to identify when it was still appropriate to offer written feedback. However, the leadership team emphasised that teachers should not assume that written feedback is always required and that it is not to be seen as the default method of providing feedback to learners. This shift of focus in the policy reduced teacher workload and improved teacher well-being while maintaining the quality of education.

PROFESSIONAL REFLECTION

Reflect on the actions that you have taken so far to address the leadership and management aspects of the Education Inspection Framework. Which aspects are you addressing well? Which aspects do you need to give greater attention to? How are you going to implement any required changes? Discuss these with a trusted colleague.

NEXT STEPS

Consider further ways that you can reduce unnecessary workload in relation to planning, data management and assessment. Look through samples of students' work to evaluate the extent to which marking is enabling learners to make further progress. Are learners reading the feedback? Are they using the feedback to make further progress in their learning? How might planning, assessment and data management be reduced?

TAKE 5

- Think carefully about the professional development needs of staff. Identify how these can be met.
- Identify what you can do to reduce unnecessary workload for teachers in relation to planning, assessment and data management.

- Reflect on how to strengthen links with parents and the wider community to develop existing relationships.

- Consider how the school takes steps to ensure that all learners complete their programmes of study.

- Identify what you can do to develop a positive school culture so that learners and staff can thrive.

WHAT HAVE YOU LEARNED?

This chapter has highlighted effective practices of leadership and management within the context of the Education Inspection Framework. In doing so, it has addressed the requirements of the inspection process in relation to this aspect of the new framework. The chapter has emphasised the importance of senior leaders committing to the provision of an ambitious curriculum and we have provided some discussion to exemplify effective practice. Additionally, the chapter has outlined leaders' responsibilities in relation to the professional development of staff. Some guidance has been provided to support leaders to understand the concepts of 'gaming' and 'off-rolling'. Within this guidance we have emphasised the importance of leaders working to ensure that all learners complete their programmes of study. The chapter then outlined leaders' responsibilities in relation to working with the community, reducing unnecessary workload and developing a positive culture. The role of school governors has been discussed, and through this discussion we have highlighted the roles and responsibilities of the governing body in relation to accountability. Practical guidance has also been offered to support leaders to develop a culture of safeguarding through reflecting on existing provision within the school context.

FURTHER READING

Buck, A (2018) *Leadership Matters 3.0: How Leaders At All Levels Can Create Great Schools.* Melton: John Catt.

Stones, S and Glazzard, J (2020) *Positive Mental Health for School Leaders.* St Albans: Critical Publishing.

8

KEY THINGS TO REMEMBER

WHAT WILL YOU LEARN?

This chapter summarises some of the key messages stated in previous chapters. It also revisits the four key aspects of the Education Inspection Framework (Ofsted, 2019) and highlights the key points for you as an early career teacher. Important guidance is provided in this chapter to support you in looking after your own mental health, and advice is offered to enable you to be resilient to the challenges that you will face. The chapter also offers some helpful tips to support you in staying organised.

KEY POLICY

This chapter focuses on all aspects of the Education Inspection Framework. The Department for Education has established an advisory group to inform policy on teacher well-being. Over the last two years the Department for Education has also produced several guidance documents on teacher workload. These are referenced in the Further Reading section.

DON'T PANIC

It might sound easy for us to say 'don't panic' when you get the Ofsted call. This phone call can ignite a range of emotions in colleagues. Some will relish the opportunity to shine in front of inspectors and others will be terrified. People will also situate themselves anywhere between these two extremes.

The important thing to remember first and foremost is that the inspection is not all about you. It is the school as a whole that is being inspected rather than the individuals within it. Of course, it is natural to some extent that you won't want to let your team down. It is likely that you will feel that you need to do well, not only to preserve your reputation as a teacher, but also to maintain your reputation with school leaders, colleagues, students and the community as a whole.

Try to relax in a stressful situation. The more you panic, the worse you will feel. No one can guarantee the outcome of an inspection. We cannot predict everything that will happen during an inspection because it is inevitable that some lessons will go well and others may not go so well. After you have been alerted about the inspection, get your lessons prepared. Discuss your lesson ideas with colleagues if necessary, but don't waste valuable time preparing 'all-singing, all-dancing' lessons. Teach the content that is identified on your medium-term planning so that you do not interrupt the sequencing of children's learning. Do not spend hours preparing elaborate resources for your lessons, particularly if this not typical. The children will give this away. Try to just teach the way you normally do. Be clear in your mind what you want the students to learn and how you will structure the lesson to ensure that they learn what you intend them to learn. Remember to build assessment opportunities into your lessons through the use of techniques such as questioning, summarising and assessment for learning tasks. These do not need to be elaborate or time-consuming to plan.

Inspectors are not looking to try to trip you up. They are looking at what you do to promote learning. They will be interested in how your lesson fits into a sequence of learning, and they may request to see your medium- or long-term planning to see how you sequence knowledge and skills over time. In this inspection framework inspectors are likely to spend more time observing the quality of education in class-rooms than has been the case in previous inspections. You do not need to waste time making your classroom look beautiful by putting up new, shiny displays. This is window-dressing and inspectors will sniff this out. Focus on planning some great lessons, relax and get some sleep so that you feel fresh for the inspection.

DON'T TREAT INSPECTORS AS THE ENEMY

Inspectors are not the enemy. They are colleagues who are tasked with doing an important job. If you are a good teacher, then inspectors will recognise this. If you feel, in your meeting with inspectors, that they have not formed an accurate view about a particular aspect of your practice, then be prepared to challenge inspectors professionally by presenting them with evidence to support your opinion. Most inspectors will interpret this positively; if you are making a strong case about some-thing, then it means that you are passionate about your job and that it matters to you.

Try to be confident when speaking to inspectors. You know your learners far better than they do. You will have formulated a clear rationale to underpin your practice and you need to be confident in articulating this. Most inspectors do not relish criticising teachers. If you are observed by an inspector and the lesson does not go well, then don't panic. They will not evaluate your teaching on the basis of a single snapshot. They will look at the quality of work in books to see if learners are making good progress over time. They will talk to pupils to ascertain what they know and can do. They will also look at your planning to check that you are planning to develop knowledge and skills cumulatively. If the full range of evidence indicates that you are a good teacher, then you do not need to panic about one lesson that does not reach expectations.

LOOKING AFTER YOUR MENTAL HEALTH

Take care of your mental health, particularly during an inspection, but also the rest of the time. Make sure that you are getting sufficient sleep, eating a healthy diet and make time to 'switch off' from work. Try to participate in physical activity and do not lose contact with your friends. Working excessive hours will not make you a better teacher.

LEARN TO BE RESILIENT

Learn to be resilient. If, during the inspection, a lesson does not go according to plan, it is not the end of the world. One poor lesson is unlikely to impact on the overall inspection judgement, particularly if the other sources of evidence indicate that you are a good teacher. Leave this lesson in the past where it belongs and move on. View feedback from inspectors on the quality of your planning, teaching and assessment as developmental rather than as a criticism. If you are having a tough time, talk to supportive colleagues, friends and members of your family. Our social connections strengthen our resilience.

BE ORGANISED

The key to success in teaching and during inspections is to stay organised. Try to keep on top of your workload so that it doesn't mount up. There will be times when keeping on top of things is difficult. Teachers have an incredibly high workload and sometimes it is impossible to complete all the jobs on your 'to do' list. There will be times when you have to prioritise some tasks over others, and there will also be times when you have to 'cut corners' to survive. You won't be able to achieve perfection in every task, although you will probably strive to do this. Sometimes 'good enough' has to be sufficient.

If you keep on top of your planning, marking and assessment records, it makes life easier when you receive the inspection call. Staying organised all the time will mean that you don't need to frantically catch up with tasks when you suddenly receive notification of an inspection. The notice period is so short that you will realistically only have time to concentrate on planning and resourcing your lessons before the inspectors arrive. Getting behind on your tasks will increase your stress levels and this is something that you will definitely want to avoid in an inspection. It will be stressful anyway, so don't make things worse than they need to be by having to play catch-up.

QUALITY OF EDUCATION

Inspectors will focus more on the quality of education that your learners receive. The Education Inspection Framework focuses specifically on the sequencing of knowledge and skills within your curriculum planning. Inspectors may ask to see long-term and medium-term plans to understand how you are sequencing learning to enable students to make progress over time. They will not want to see a lesson plan, but they will be interested in how you choose to order learning, specifically in relation to how you plan to revisit knowledge and skills over time to ensure that they transfer into the long-term memory.

Inspectors will evaluate the quality of education through:

- intent – the quality of the curriculum;

- implementation – the quality of the teaching;

- impact – gains in knowledge, skills, attainment and qualifications.

When you are observed by inspectors, it is likely that they will focus on the accuracy of your subject knowledge. They will be interested in how clearly you explain subject content and how well you use assessment during lessons to check learners' understanding. Using questioning effectively will enable you to check understanding, identify misconceptions and respond to these during lessons. Don't be afraid to adapt the lesson to respond to the needs of your learners if they are developing misconceptions. Questioning should also be used to promote deeper thinking or to scaffold students' understanding. Building in short assessment tasks throughout the lesson will enable you to ascertain whether your learners have understood and whether you can move on with the lesson. Summarising the learning at specific points during the lesson supports students' understanding by reminding them of the key subject content. Inspectors will check the way in which you feed back to learners during lessons so that they know how well they have done. The use of oral feedback throughout lessons is particularly important, as is the use of live marking within lessons. In addition, the use of live assessment during lessons by modelling correct responses on the board, screen or using the visualiser is also an effective strategy because it ensures that learners understand the expected standard.

Inspectors are not looking for a 'model' of teaching. You can use a variety of approaches for structuring lessons, but essentially the lesson structure should support learners' progress. Inspectors will certainly not be looking for the use of specific lesson features to be present. Your lesson may not have a traditional starter or plenary, for example. Inspectors will not expect to see a particular teaching style. You may decide to lead the lesson more from the front. Alternatively, you may include more group work or independent work in the lesson. You might decide to use a mixture of these approaches. Inspectors will not make judgements on the amount of 'teacher talk' that takes place during lessons. Whatever style of teaching you adopt, inspectors will only be interested in the impact that your teaching has on learners' knowledge, skills, confidence and attitudes. Learners do not have to be 'doing' activities to be actively engaged in the lesson. They might be actively engaged in thinking things through and problem solving. Inspectors will be interested in the pace of learning during the lesson, but it is important to remember that cramming too many activities into lessons can over-complicate things and reduce the pace of learning because learners only have a short time allocated for each task. Pace of learning is not about the number of activities that you ask your learners to do or the time you spend on each activity. It is about depth of learning. You can achieve depth of learning through focusing on one thing rather than on many.

BEHAVIOUR AND ATTITUDES

Inspectors will be interested in learners' behaviour and attitudes both in lessons and around the school. They will check that learners conduct themselves appropriately by attending lessons, being punctual and settling straight down to work. They will be interested in their attitudes to learning and their broader education. These include the following.

- Do they ask questions?

- Do they challenge you or each other appropriately if they disagree?

- Do they persevere with difficult tasks until they complete them?

- Can they work independently and stay focused?

- Do they maintain concentration when they are listening to you or their peers?

- Do they regulate their behaviour?

- Is there any bullying?

- Are they polite and respectful to others?

- Are they resilient to setbacks?

The important thing is to ensure that these attitudes to learning and education are consistently reinforced. These attitudes need to be established from the start of the academic year so that learners understand what is expected of them. You cannot expect them to suddenly demonstrate these attitudes during an inspection if these expectations have not been consistently reinforced throughout the year.

CASE STUDY

A primary school wanted to create a more positive school culture to address the strand of *Behaviour and Attitudes* in the Education Inspection Framework. Teachers planned a diversity week to address the themes of disability, race and LGBTQ+ identities. Creative activities were planned and pupils wrote poems, created artwork, performed drama, read stories and completed a photography project. These activities deepened the children's understanding of diversity. The overarching theme for the week was 'promoting respect'. The themes of race, disability and sexuality were also embedded into the history curriculum.

PERSONAL DEVELOPMENT

Inspectors will explore students' resilience, character and independence during lessons. They will also talk to students about how the school promotes their understanding of mental health and health education. Through talking to students, inspectors will explore their understanding of the fundamental British values. They will also observe students out of class to monitor these aspects of their development. In addition, inspectors may check curriculum plans, particularly in relation to character, citizenship education and mental health, to explore how knowledge, skills and attitudes are developed cumulatively.

CASE STUDY

A secondary school focused on the theme of digital citizenship. A scheme of work was developed for students in Year 8 to support them in understanding what it means to be a good digital citizen. Students studied this theme through a range of learning experiences. These included analysing written case studies, examining online content and learning about the law. They were introduced to key research which examines the association between social media and mental health. They were taught how to report instances of online abuse and how to be digitally resilient.

LEADERSHIP AND MANAGEMENT

Inspectors will evaluate the quality of leadership through forming judgements about how effectively the school meets its legal safeguarding duties. In addition, inspectors will be interested in the vision for the school curriculum. This is a new focus for inspection. Inspectors will evaluate the extent to which leaders promote staff well-being through reducing unnecessary workload, protecting staff from bullying and providing staff with high-quality, tailored professional development. The emphasis on staff well-being is a new focus for inspection. Inspectors will evaluate the quality of the schools' extra-curricular offer and the partnerships which have been established with the community.

YOU ARE ON A JOURNEY

As an early career teacher, you are on a lifelong journey of development. You are never the finished product. Good teachers continue to reflect on their practice and develop as teachers. Don't beat yourself up about this. You will make mistakes. This is a normal aspect of teacher development. View teaching as an ongoing journey of development rather than as a need to reach a final destination and enjoy the ride.

KEY RESEARCH

Research shows that, although effective teachers use a significant amount of teacher talk in their classes, most of it is focused on subject content, and much of it involves asking questions and giving feedback rather than extended lecturing (Kyriakides and Creemers, 2008). This supports learners to process information actively.

PROFESSIONAL REFLECTION

Reflect on your own approach to organisation and time management. What are your strengths? What are your weaknesses? Reflect on whether any of your work-related tasks are unnecessary? Which tasks are essential and which tasks could you stop doing? Which tasks could you do differently to save time?

NEXT STEPS

Talk to colleagues in school about their experiences of inspection. Find out how they prepare for inspections and how they survived them.

TAKE 5

- Keep on top of your workload. Try not to let tasks mount up.

- Establish expectations for learners' behaviour from the beginning of the academic year.

- Less is sometimes more; don't cram too much into your lessons.

- Build assessment into your lessons.

- Don't be afraid to adapt your lessons to respond to the needs of your learners.

WHAT HAVE YOU LEARNED?

This chapter has emphasised the essential points from the Education Inspection Framework. It has provided clear guidance on what inspectors will be looking for when they observe lessons. It has emphasised the critical role of assessment within your teaching and also stressed that inspectors will not expect to see a specific model of teaching.

FURTHER READING

Policy advice on reducing teacher workload can be found on the following website:

www.gov.uk/guidance/school-workload-reduction-toolkit

The following documents are also useful:

Department for Education (DfE) (2018) *Ways to Reduce Workload in Your School(s): Tips and Case Studies from School Leaders, Teachers and Sector Experts*. London: DfE.

Department for Education (DfE) (2018) *Addressing Teacher Workload in Initial Teacher Education (ITE): Advice for ITE Providers*. London: DfE.

Department for Education (DfE) (2019) *Reducing Workload: Supporting Teachers in the Early Stages of Their Career Advice for School Leaders, Induction Tutors, Mentors and Appropriate Bodies*. London: DfE.

Workload Review Group (2016a) *Eliminating Unnecessary Workload Around Marking: Report of the Independent Teacher Workload Review Group.* London: Department for Education. Crown copyright.

Workload Review Group (2016b) *Eliminating Unnecessary Worklo*

ad Around Planning and Teaching Resources: Report of the Independent Teacher Workload Review Group. London: Department for Education. Crown copyright.

Workload Review Group (2016c) *Eliminating Unnecessary Workload Associated with Data Management Report of the Independent Teacher Workload Review Group.* London: Department for Education. Crown copyright.

9

CONCLUSION

This book has outlined the key components of the Education Inspection Framework (Ofsted, 2019) and the implications of this framework for you as a teacher. We have emphasised the importance of placing limits on your workload, particularly in relation to tasks that don't help learners to make progress.

The new emphasis on the quality of education provides schools with an exciting opportunity to plan and implement a rich, creative and exciting curriculum that meets the needs of learners and the communities that schools serve. It provides you with permission to plan a broad and inspiring curriculum that provides students with deep learning opportunities. The focus on a curriculum that provides learners with cultural capital should ensure that all young people can access the same life opportunities regardless of their social background or other circumstances.

The challenge for teachers is that although there is a renewed focus on learners' entitlement to a broad curriculum, academic outcomes in priority subjects will continue to be taken into consideration. There is an assumption that a rich, broad and exciting curriculum will result in improved academic outcomes. However, there is a potential risk that schools may invest in rich curriculum opportunities, but struggle to demonstrate impact through academic outcomes in the subjects that are being nationally assessed. It remains to be seen if these schools will be praised for the quality of their curriculum offer if academic outcomes in priority subjects are not in line with national standards.

The 'deep dives' that will form part of the inspection process will enable inspectors to focus on the quality of the curriculum, teaching and depth of learning in specific subjects. Deep dives will include subjects that are not nationally assessed. This strategy should ensure that schools are giving greater attention to subjects that are not nationally assessed. However, there is a danger that this approach will simply create more work for teachers who are already struggling to keep on top of their workloads.

The role of assessment in promoting learning is an integral part of effective teaching and is embedded in the new inspection framework. Inspectors will focus on how effectively teachers use assessment in the lesson to enable learners to make progress rather than focusing on internal assessment data which has been characteristic of previous inspection frameworks.

The focus on learners' personal development is a welcome component of the new framework. It is refreshing to see that inspectors will evaluate the school's approach to mental and physical health, and the effectiveness of the school's inclusion strategy. Character education and citizenship education are the bedrock of a civilised society and the emphasis on these aspects is a positive development. At the same time, it must be remembered that schools should not be made responsible for solving all of society's problems. It is also important to remember that teachers are fundamentally responsible for education and that they are not health professionals. Placing duties on teachers to identify the signs and symptoms of mental ill health changes the role of the teacher and potentially makes them vulnerable in cases where they 'fail' to spot the signs of mental illness. It is not fair to place teachers in this position. In addition, although schools can and do play a role in supporting young people's mental health, shifting the responsibility on to schools for mental health simply absolves the government from addressing the systemic factors that are the root causes of mental ill health. These include poverty, adverse childhood experiences and an increasingly academic curriculum and assessment system that do not meet the needs of all learners. These systemic factors necessitate a political response and teachers are not in a position to reduce their effects.

It is refreshing that the judgement on leadership and management will evaluate the extent to which school leaders have made attempts to reduce unnecessary workload for teachers and whether leaders have subjected specific members of staff to bullying. Leaders need to look after their teachers because they are the school's greatest asset. Teachers who are trusted to do their jobs, valued and provided with autonomy are more likely to be mentally healthy and do a good job. Toxic school cultures, in which staff and learners are subjected to bullying, are not good environments in which to learn and work. Every member of the school community should experience a sense of belonging. If the framework eradicates bullying and off-rolling, then it will play a critical role in the development of more inclusive schools.

Inspection is nothing to worry about. As we have stated in this book, if you are doing a good job, then inspectors will recognise this. Try to treat inspectors as colleagues rather than 'the enemy' and be prepared to challenge them in discussions if they make inaccurate judgements about your work. Inspectors will generally see this as a sign of strength and an indicator that you are passionate about your work.

Schools are well-placed to address the requirements of the new framework. However, there are also important implications for programmes of initial teacher education. It is important that teacher education programmes provide trainee teachers with the skills that they need so that they can thrive in the classroom. Just as schools are having to review their curriculum offer, so too must teacher education providers. Providers should ensure that trainee teachers understand how to properly sequence learning so that learners develop knowledge and skills cumulatively. Providers should also ensure that primary trainees have extensive, rich and deep opportunities to develop knowledge and skills in the foundation subjects, and trainees need to understand how knowledge and skills in one subject can be applied in other subjects so that learners make meaningful links between subjects. In addition, trainees need to understand how to assess learning in the foundation subjects and how to use assessment effectively in lessons to enable learners to make progress. In both primary and secondary programmes, providers need to help trainee teachers to understand how to plan a curriculum that provides learners with cultural capital. Teacher education programmes need to provide more practical training on behaviour management and trainees need to be provided with practical tasks through which they learn to address the challenges associated with teaching. These include managing heavy workloads, being resilient and working with difficult parents. Some of the traditional learning theories need to be displaced from courses of initial teacher education so that trainees can learn about developing memory and cognitive neuroscience. Teacher education needs to keep pace with the changes that are happening in schools. If it fails to do this, the next generation of teachers will not be prepared to teach the curriculum offer that is available in schools, and they will not be able to address the numerous challenges that are associated with the job of being a teacher.

REFERENCES

Allen, R and Thomson, D (2016) *Changing the Subject: How are the EBacc and Attainment 8 reforms changing results?* London: The Sutton Trust.

Barenberg, J, Roeder, UR and Dutke, S (2018) Students' temporal distributing of learning activities in psychology courses: factors of influence and effects on the metacognitive learning outcome. *Psychology Learning and Teaching*, 17 (3): 257–71.

Barnes, J and Scoffham, S (2017) The humanities in English primary schools: struggling to survive. *Education*, 45 (3): 3–13.

Baumert, J, Kunter, M, Blum, W, Brunner, M, Voss, T, Jordan, A and Tsai, YM (2010) Teachers' mathematical knowledge, cognitive activation in the classroom, and student progress. *American Educational Research Journal*, 47 (1): 133–80.

Beltman, S, Mansfield, C and Price, A (2011) Thriving, not just surviving: a review of research on teacher resilience. *Educational Research Review*, 6 (3): 185–207.

Berliner, D (2011) Rational responses to high stakes testing: the case of curriculum narrowing and the harm that follows. *Cambridge Journal of Education*, 41 (3): 287–302.

Biesta, G (2009) Good education in an age of measurement: on the need to reconnect with the question of purpose in education. *Educational Assessment, Evaluation and Accountability*, 21 (1): 33–46.

Black, P and Wiliam, D (1998) Inside the black box: raising standards through classroom assessment. *Phi Delta Kappa*, 80 (2): 139–44, 146–8.

Brophy, J and Good, TL (1986) Teacher behavior and student achievement, in Wittrock, MC (ed.) *Handbook of Research on Teaching* (3rd edn). New York; London: Macmillan, pp328–75.

Brown, S and Taylor, K (2008) Bullying, education and earnings: evidence from the National Child Development Study. *Economics of Education Review*, 27 (4): 387–401.

Buckingham, J, Wheldall, K and Beams-Wheldall, R (2013) Why Jaydon can't read: the triumph of ideology over evidence in teaching reading. *Policy*, 29 (3), 21–32.

Calear, AL and Christensen, H (2010) Systematic review of school-based prevention and early intervention programs for depression. *Journal of Adolescence*, 33 (3): 429–38.

Campos, L, Dias, P, Duarte, A, Veiga, E, Camila Dias, C and Palh, F (2018) Is it possible to 'find space for mental health' in young people? Effectiveness of a school-based mental health literacy promotion program. *International Journal of Environmental Research and Public Health*, 1: 1–12.

Coe, R, Aloisi, C, Higgins, S and Major, LE (2014) *What Makes Great Teaching? Review of the Underpinning Research*. London: Sutton Trust.

Cordingley, P, Higgins, S, Greany, T, Buckler, N, Coles-Jordan, D, Crisp, B, Coe, R, Saunders, L and Greany, T (2015) Developing great teaching – lessons from the international reviews into effective professional development. London: Teacher Development Trust.

Corrigan, P and Watson, A (2007) How children stigmatize people with mental illness. *International Journal of Social Psychiatry*, 53: 526–46.

Creemers, BPM (1994) *The Effective Classroom.* London: Cassell.

Creemers, BPM and Kyriakides, L (2008) Critical analysis of the current approaches to modelling educational effectiveness: the importance of establishing a dynamic model. *School Effectiveness and School Improvement*, 17(3): 347–66.

Day, C, Sammons, P, Hopkins, D, Harris, A, Leithwood, K, Gu, Q and Brown, E (2010) 10 strong claims about successful school leadership. Nottingham: National College for School Leadership.

Department for Education (DfE) (2011) *Teachers' Standards Guidance for School Leaders, School Staff and Governing Bodies.* London: DfE.

Department for Education (DfE) (2013) Citizenship programmes of study: key stages 3 and 4. Available online at: https://assets.publishing.service.gov.uk/government/uploads/system/uploads/attachment_data/file/239060/SECONDARY_national_curriculum_-_Citizenship.pdf (accessed 24 November 2019).

Department for Education (DfE) (2015) Citizenship. Available online at: https://assets.publishing.service.gov.uk/government/uploads/system/uploads/attachment_data/file/402173/Programme_of_Study_KS1_and_2.pdf (accessed 24 November 2019).

Department for Education (DfE) (2017) *Case Studies of Behaviour Management Practices in Schools Rated Outstanding.* London: DfE.

Department for Education (DfE)/Department of Health (DoH) (2017) Transforming children and young people's mental health provision: a Green Paper, December. Crown copyright. Available online at: https://assets.publishing.service.gov.uk/government/uploads/system/uploads/attachment_data/file/664855/Transforming_children_and_young_people_s_mental_health_provision.pdf (accessed 11 June 2019).

Department for Education (DfE) (2019a) *Character Education Framework Guidance.* London: DfE.

Department for Education (DfE) (2019b) *Keeping Children Safe in Education: Statutory Guidance for Schools and Colleges.* London: DfE.

Desforges, C (2003) The impact of parental involvement, parental support and family education on pupil achievements and adjustment: a literature review. Research Report RR433. London: DfES.

Deunk, MI, Smale-Jacobse, AE, de-Boer, H, Doolaardand, S and Bosker, RJ (2018) Effective differentiation practices: a systematic review and meta-analysis of studies on the cognitive effects of differentiation practices in primary education. *Educational Research Review*, 24 (1): 31–54.

Durlak, JA, Weissberg, R, Dymnicki, A, Taylor, R and Schellinger, K (2014) The impact of enhancing students' social and emotional learning: a meta-analysis of school-based universal interventions. *Child Development*, 82 (1): 405–32.

Education Support Partnership (ESP) (2019) *Teacher Wellbeing Index, 2019.* London: ESP.

Ehren, MCM, Gustafsson, JE, Altricher, J, Skedsmo, D, Kemethofer, D and Huber, SG (2015) Comparing effects and side effects of different school inspection systems across Europe. *Comparative Education*, 51 (3): 375–400.

Equality Act (2010) Protected characteristics. Available online at: www.legislation.gov.uk/ukpga/2010/15/pdfs/ukpga_20100015_en.pdf (accessed 24 November 2018).

Fonagy, P, Twemlow, SW, Vernberg, E, Sacco, FC and Little, TD (2005) Creating a peaceful school learning environment: the impact of an antibullying program on educational attainment in elementary schools. *Medical Science Monitor*, 11 (3): 317–s25.

Frith, E (2017) *Social Media and Children's Mental Health: A Review of the Evidence*. London: Education Policy Institute.

Glazzard, J (2019) A whole-school approach to supporting children and young people's mental health. *Journal of Public Mental Health*, 18 (4): 10.

Glazzard, J and Stones, S (2019) *Social Media and Young People's Mental Health. Technology and Child Mental Health*, IntechOpen. DOI: 10.5772/intechopen.88569

Glazzard, J, Rose, A and Ogilvie, P (2019) The impact of peer mentoring on students' physical activity and mental health. *Journal of Public Mental Health*.

Goodman, A, Joshi, H, Nasim, B and Tyler, C (2015) *Social and Emotional Skills in Childhood and Their Long-term Effects on Adult Life*. London: UCL.

Hattie, J (2009) *Visible Learning: A Synthesis of Over 800 Meta-analysis Relating to Achievement*. London: Routledge.

Hattie, J and Timperley, H (2007) The power of feedback. *Review of Educational Research*, 77 (1): 81–112.

Higgins, S and Katsipataki, M (2015) Evidence from meta-analysis about parental involvement in education which supports their children's learning. *Journal of Children's Services*, 10 (3): 280–90.

Jones, K, Tymms, P, Kemethofer, D, O'Hara, J, McNamara, G, Huber, S, Myrberg, E, Skedsmo, G and Greger, D (2017) The unintended consequences of school inspection: the prevalence of inspection side-effects in Austria, the Czech Republic, England, Ireland, the Netherlands, Sweden, and Switzerland. *Oxford Review of Education*, 43 (6): 805–22.

Jorm, A, Korten, A, Jacomb, P, Christensen, H, Rodgers, B and Pollitt, P (1997) Mental health literacy: a survey of the public's ability to recognise mental disorders and their beliefs about the effectiveness of treatment. *Medical Journal of Australia*, 166: 182–6.

Jorm, AF, Barney, LJ, Christensen, H, Highet, NJ, Kelly, CM and Kitchener, BA (2006) Research on mental health literacy: what we know and what we still need to know. *Australian and New Zealand Journal of Psychiatry*, 40: 3–5.

Kelly, CM, Jorm, AF and Wright, A (2007) Improving mental health literacy as a strategy to facilitate early intervention for mental disorders. *Medical Journal of Australia*, 187: 26–30.

Kyriakides, L and Creemers, BPM (2008) A longitudinal study on the stability over time of school and teacher effects on student outcomes. *Oxford Review of Education*, 34 (5): 521–45.

Martínez-Zambrano, F, García-Morales, E, García-Franco, M, Miguel, J, Villellas, R, Pascual, G, Arenas, O and Ochoa, S (2013) Intervention for reducing stigma: assessing the influence of gender and knowledge. *World Journal of Psychiatry*, 18–24.

Maslow, AH (1943) A theory of human motivation. *Psychological Review*, 50 (4): 370–96.

Muijs, D and Reynolds, D (2003) Student background and teacher effects on achievement and attainment in mathematics: a longitudinal study. *Educational Research and Evaluation*, 9 (3): 289–314.

Office for Standards in Education (Ofsted) (2002) The curriculum in successful primary schools. Available online at: http://dera.ioe.ac.uk/4564/1/Curriculum%20in%20success-ful%20primary%20schools%20%28The%29%20%28PDF%20format%29.pdf (accessed 26 November 2019).

Office for Standards in Education (Ofsted) (2018) Ofsted inspection – clarification for schools. Available online at: https://assets.publishing.service.gov.uk/government/uploads/system/uploads/attachment_data/file/730129/Ofsted_inspections_-_clarification_for_schools_270718.pdf

Office for Standards in Education (Ofsted) (2019) Education Inspection Framework: Overview of Research. Manchester: Ofsted.

Polesel, J, Rice, S and Dulfer, N (2014) The impact of high-stakes testing on curriculum and pedagogy: a teacher perspective from Australia. *Journal of Education Policy*, 29 (5): 640–57.

Public Health England (PHE) (2015) *Promoting Children and Young People's Emotional Health and Wellbeing: A Whole School and College Approach*. London: PHE.

Rawson, A and Kintsch, W (2005) Rereading effects depend on time of test. *Journal of Educational Psychology*, 97 (1): 70–80.

Reynolds, D, Sammons, S, De Fraine, B, Van Damme, J, Townsend, T, Teddlie, C and Stringfield, S (2014) Educational effectiveness research (EER): a state-of-the-art review. *School Effectiveness and School Improvement*, 25 (2):197–230.

Richland, LE, Bjork, RA, Finley, JR and Linn, MC (2005) Linking cognitive science to education: generation and interleaving effects. In Bara, BG, Barsalou, L and Bucciarelli, M (eds) *Proceedings of the Twenty-Seventh Annual Conference of the Cognitive Science Society*. Mahwah, NJ: Lawrence Erlbaum.

Roediger, HL and Karpicke, JD (2006) Test-enhanced learning: taking memory tests improves long-term retention. *Psychological Science*, 17 (3): 249–55.

Roffey, S (2017) Ordinary magic needs ordinary magicians: the power and practice of positive relationships for building youth resilience and wellbeing. *Kognition und Paedagogik*, 103: 38–57.

Rohrer, D, Dedrick, R and Stershic, S (2015) Interleaved practice improves mathematics learning. *Journal of Educational Psychology*, 107 (3): 900–8.

Rosenshine, B (2010) *Principles of Instruction*. International Academy of Education, UNESCO. Geneva: International Bureau of Education.

Rosenshine, B (2012) Principles of instruction: research based strategies that all teachers should know. *American Educator*, 36 (1): 12–19.

Rosenshine, B and Stevens, R (1986) Teaching functions. In Wittrock, MC (ed.) *Handbook of Research on Teaching* (3rd edn). New York; London: Macmillan, pp376–91.

Scheerens, J and Bosker, R (1997) *The Foundations of Educational Effectiveness*. Pergamon.

Seidel, T and Shavelson, RJ (2007) Teaching effectiveness research in the past decade: the role of theory and research design in disentangling meta-analysis results. *Review of Educational Research*, 77 (4): 454–99.

Sharples, J, Webster, R and Blatchford, P (2015) *Making Best Use of Teaching Assistants Guidance Report*. London: Education Endowment Foundation.

Shochet, IM, Dadds, MR, Ham, D and Montague, R (2006) School connectedness is an under-emphasised parameter in adolescent mental health: results of a community prediction study. *Journal of Clinical Child and Adolescent Psychology*, 35 (2): 170–9.

Siraj-Blatchford, I, Sylva, K, Muttock, S, Gilden, R and Bell, D (2002) Researching Effective Pedagogy in the Early Years (REPEY): DfES Research Report 356. Norwich: HMSO.

Skinner, BF (1938) *The Behaviour of Organisms: An Experimental Analysis*. Oxford: Appleton-Century.

Smith, F, Hardman, F, Wall, K and Mroz, M (2004) Interactive whole class teaching in the National Numeracy and Literacy Strategies. *British Educational Research Journal*, 30 (3): 395–411.

Smith, L and Land, M (1981) Low-inference verbal behaviors related to teacher clarity. *Journal of Classroom Interaction*, 17: 37–42.

Spielman, A (2019) Amanda Spielman, Ofsted's Chief Inspector, introduces the new framework. Available online at: www.youtube.com/watch?v=byaUliCMi9E

Stallings, J (1985) Effective elementary classroom practices. In Kyle, MJ (ed.) *Reaching for Excellence: An Effective Sourcebook*. Washington, DC: US Governing Printing Office.

Sweller, J (2011) Cognitive load theory. *Psychology of Learning and Motivation*, 55: 37–76.

Walberg, HJ (1986) Syntheses of research on teaching. In Wittrock, MC (ed.) *Handbook of Research on Teaching* (3rd edn). New York: Macmillan, pp 214–29.

Wayne, A and Youngs, P (2003) Teacher characteristics and student achievement gains: a review. *Review of Educational Research*, 73 (1): 89–122.

World Health Organization (WHO) (2004) Mental health: a state of well-being. Available online at: www.who.int/features/factfiles/mental_health/en/ (accessed 22 November 2019).

Young, M (2013) Overcoming the crisis in curriculum theory: a knowledge based approach. *Journal of Curriculum Studies*, 45 (2): 101–18.

INDEX